Practical Handbook to Elementary Foreign Language Programs

Practical Handbook to Elementary Foreign Language Programs

Including FLES, FLEX, and Immersion Programs

Gladys C. Lipton

 National Textbook Company • Lincolnwood, Illinois U.S.A.

DEDICATION

This book is dedicated to children all over the world who have known the joy of learning another language in the elementary or primary school.

This book is also dedicated to four very special children: Lorrie, Jeremy, Seth, and Rachel.

ACKNOWLEDGMENTS

I should like to express appreciation to the hundreds of FLES and secondary-school foreign language teachers with whom I have worked over the years. I am grateful for the intellectual stimulation they have provided as well as the warm friendships that have developed.

I am particularly thankful to my husband, Robert Lipton, for his patience, his encouragement, and his tremendous support of this project as well as the many other endeavors I have undertaken.

I am indebted to Michael Ross, Senior Foreign Language Editor at National Textbook Company, for his expertise, assistance, and encouragement, and to Charles Liebowitz, Vice President of NTC, for having had the vision to support my writing of this book.

Finally, I would like to thank my first foreign language methods teacher at Brooklyn College (New York City), who first introduced me to the attractions of FLES by scheduling a class visit to a Grade 4 French FLES class in a nearby elementary school. Little did I know then that that visit would be the initial thrust in my exciting career as a FLES teacher for more than seven years, secondary school foreign language teacher, coordinator and supervisor (K–12), doctoral student, author, director, teacher-trainer in FLES and secondary school methods, workshop presenter, keynote speaker—who knows what else!

GLADYS C. LIPTON

Contents

Practical Handbook to Elementary Foreign Language Programs

Introduction

WHAT IS FLES*?

The world is changing. Technology is changing. Educational programs are also changing—and **FLES** programs are changing, too. But the basic premise of introducing children to one or more foreign languages (and cultures) has been with us a long time. And yet, each new generation of parents and teachers redis- covers the enormous educational and intercultural value of an early start in the study of foreign languages.

In the fifties and sixties, **FLES** programs dealt with dia- logues and songs about candy, crayons, and colors. These simple topics are not sufficiently interesting to today's generation of children, who have become blasé about intergalactic travel and interstellar communication. Not surprisingly, though, **FLES** pro- grams have endured, have been revived and reinstated, have developed new approaches and styles, have become important as an interdisciplinary approach to elementary school education, and have branched out to offer new and exciting options. Op- tions to receive attention in this handbook are:

---

*When we print **FLES** like this, in bold type—or in headings like this, **FLES***, in bold type followed by an asterisk—we are using it as the overall term for any foreign language program in the elementary grades. This should help prevent confusing it with the program option called FLES, or sequential FLES. This unfortunate duplication of terms in the discipline will only be solved by the profession.

1. **FLES**   Foreign Language in the Elementary School, kindergarten through grade 6 (sometimes called sequential, revitalized, traditional, or standard FLES).

2. **FLEX**   Foreign Language Experience or Exploratory, kindergarten through grade 6 (*Note: "Exploratory" is also used to describe a multilanguage course in the middle schools*): an early introduction to one or more foreign languages and cultures; sometimes called a language awareness or cultural awareness program.

3. **Immersion** (or **partial immersion**)   kindergarten through grade 6: foreign language used as the language of instruction through all or most of the school day.

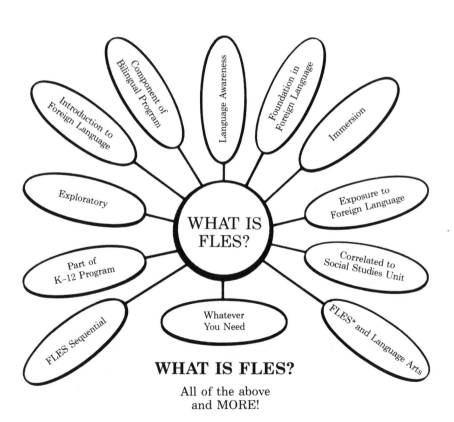

WHAT IS FLES?

All of the above
and MORE!

These basic types of **FLES** (and various modifications and combinations) are represented by the overall term **FLES—F**oreign **L**anguage in **E**lementary **S**chool.

DIFFERENT TYPES OF FLES*

FLES

This type of program permits a wide variety of formats and time and scheduling patterns, and has as its major focus the teaching of one language for two school years or more. The goal is to provide instruction in the four skills: listening and understanding, speaking, reading, and writing, as well as cultural awareness. The sequential FLES program attempts to provide a long exposure to one foreign language, with the expectation of some degree of proficiency, usually built on chosen themes that are developed during the sequential FLES curriculum. After the initial year, some student selection may be necessary, because of additional use of reading and writing activities. (Note: FLES is sometimes called "sequential," "revitalized," "intensive," etc.)

FLEX

Also called exploratory or language awareness or cultural awareness, this type of program also permits a wide variety of formats and time and scheduling patterns. It has as its major focus the teaching of one or more languages (and cultures) for one or more school years. It emphasizes exposure to more than one language and culture, with an orientation of cross-cultural contrasts. It is considered a minimal foundation in language learning, with the goal of very limited proficiency in one or more languages studied. There is usually a high level of interest, and if continued for more than one year, all or most students want to stay in the program. It is primarily a language/culture motivational program.

Immersion (and Partial Immersion)

This model is instruction in the foreign language for at least 50 percent of the school day—in total immersion, close to 100 percent. The goal is to achieve functional proficiency for students who stay with the program, while achieving normally in all the subjects taught in the foreign language. It is an integral part of the elementary school day, as the foreign language is the language of communication and instruction. There is some variety of formats (depending on the degree of immersion in the model), and English is introduced in different grades in the program (usually in grade 3). The amount of English is increased, so that by sixth grade the day is usually 50 percent English and 50 percent foreign language, although the ratio will vary from program to program. In many ways, the immersion model follows the bilingual model developed in the 1960s and 1970s in high language-minority localities in the U.S. and in Canada. Following is a chart showing the three basic types of programs of **FLES**.

Types of FLES Programs

FLES	FLEX (Exploratory, Language Awareness)	Immersion and Partial Immersion
One language, taught for two school years or more	One or more languages taught for one or more school years	One language, K–6
Grades K–6	*Grades K–6*	*Grades K–6*
Foundation language learning in four skills and culture*	Minimal foundation; language learning in four skills and culture* (sometimes only oral skills)	Subject matter of elementary school curriculum taught in the FL
Outcomes:	*Outcomes:*	*Outcomes:*
Limited proficiency	Very limited proficiency	Proficiency in the foreign language
Interest in language and culture(s)	Interest in language(s) and culture(s)	Interest in language and culture
Interest in future FL study	Interest in future FL study	Interest in study of other FL's
Correlation of FL with social studies and language arts	Correlation of FL with social studies and language arts	High correlation with social studies and language arts

Types of FLES Programs (continued)

FLES	FLEX (Exploratory, Language Awareness)	Immersion and Partial Immersion
Integral part of elementary school curriculum	Possibly integral part of elementary school curriculum	Integral part of elementary school curriculum
Teachers:	*Teachers:*	*Teachers:*
Specialist or nonspecialist	Specialist, nonspecialist, volunteers	Specialist in FL and E.S.
Students:	*Students:*	*Students:*
Available to all; some selection due to budget	Available to all students the first year	Available to limited number of students who can cope with challenge
Materials:	*Materials:*	*Materials:*
Wide variety to support content and interest	Wide variety to support content and interest	Wide variety to support content and interest
Content:	*Content:*	*Content:*
Thematic units such as greetings, health, sports, food, etc.; cultural themes	Thematic units with limited vocabulary and structure; cultural themes	Content of social studies, science, mathematics, etc.
Time:	*Time:*	*Time:*
Wide range of time based on local needs, finances, and grade levels (range from 5% to 20%)	Wide range of time based on local needs, finances, and grade levels (range from 2% to 5%)	50% to 100%

*Four skills: listening, speaking, reading, writing

Although it is difficult to get statistics on a national basis, I conducted a survey on **FLES** in 1986 by contacting the state specialists in foreign language. The results indicated that all types of sequential FLES and FLEX were reported in an overwhelming number of school districts where **FLES** was offered. Immersion and partial immersion were reported in well under 5 percent of the school districts that responded. In a national survey conducted by the Center for Language Education and Research Center for Applied Linguistics, 98 percent of those respondents who had FLES programs reported having various forms of FLES- and FLEX-type programs.*

HIGHLIGHTS

- **FLES* is the overall term for foreign language in the elementary school**

- **FLES refers to a sequential type of FL program in elementary school**

- **FLEX is a limited language experience (exploratory) program**

- ***Immersion* is a program in which the foreign language is the language of the elementary school program**

---

*Oxford, R., and N. Rhodes. *Executive Summary: Status of U.S. Foreign Language Instruction at the Elementary and Secondary School Levels.* Washington, D.C.: Center for Language Education and Research, Center for Applied Linguistics, 1987.

II

Why FLES?

WHY FLES*?

Many people find it difficult to understand that the question "Why **FLES**?" is still being asked. In the fifties and sixties, which was the heyday for standard FLES programs, parents and administrators were easily convinced that an early introduction to a foreign language for young children was worthwhile, interesting, important, and even chic! Toward the end of the sixties, taxpayers began to look for ways to cut budgets, and then all kinds of questions were asked. Some of the responses, many of which are still valid today, follow.

- Children enjoy learning a foreign language.

- Children are curious about strange sounds and secret codes.

- Children are excellent mimics.

- Children are less self-conscious about pronouncing strange sounds than are adolescents or adults.

- Children do not generally object to repetition and drill.

- Children, because of their ability to imitate so well, are capable of developing good habits of listening and correct pronunciation from **FLES** teachers, who insist upon high standards of oral skills.

- Children, by starting second language study early, are facilitated in the development of an intelligent understanding of language concepts in general, and this will help in learning additional languages.

- Children benefit from a longer sequence of language study.
- Children develop a firm foundation for continuing language study.
- Children enjoy correlating the study of a foreign language with other areas of the elementary school curriculum.
- Children begin to master the sound system of the foreign language and develop a feeling of "at-homeness" with the language.
- Children gain a cultural awareness of the foreign language and the people who speak it.
- Children are open and receptive to cross-cultural exploration.
- Children who start earlier have more time to develop functional proficiency in later years.
- Some research studies indicate that those students who studied a foreign language in grades 4, 5, and 6 achieved higher scores on standardized tests in English and mathematics. (See the Bibliography: Lipton, 119, 120; Masciantonio, 135; Oneto, 157; Rafferty, 166.)
- There is some evidence that students who study a foreign language in the elementary grades gain cognitive benefits, such as mental flexibility, creativity, and divergent thinking and problem solving. (See the Bibliography: Landry, 100, 101)
- The study of a foreign language in the grades does not interfere with normal expected progress in the other elementary school subjects. This is true for FLES and FLEX as well as immersion. (See the Bibliography: Lipton, 110; Lopato, 126; Rafferty, 166)
- In the area of attitudinal factors, studies have shown that the early introduction of a foreign language tends to break down the "monocultural" outlook of youngsters. (See the Bibliography: Lambert and Tucker, 99)
- Some early studies indicated that **FLES** had a favorable effect on foreign language study later on in high school and college.

(See the Bibliography: Brega and Newell, 27; Carroll, 31; Dunkel and Pillet, 51; Somerville, 188; and Vocolo, 212)

Over the years, parents, educators, researchers, early childhood specialists, and others have endorsed the concept that the best time to introduce foreign languages is when the child is young, before the language and speech patterns are fixed, probably before the age of eleven, as Wilder Penfield (163), a Canadian neuropsychologist, put it. Krashen and others (96) agree that children starting early excel in pronunciation of the foreign language.

Some other contemporary compelling reasons are expressed in this way:

- **FLES** (or its other options) promotes appreciation and understanding of other cultures.
- **FLES** serves as an intellectual challenge for children.
- Pronunciation is more easily learned in the early years.
- A longer sequence of language learning ensures greater proficiency at high school and college levels.
- **FLES** improves students' command of English through crossover derivations and contrasts.
- **FLES** is consistent with the educational trends of the times to offer students more basic subjects.
- **FLES** promotes closer ties with members of the community, particularly if the language being taught is spoken by members of the community.
- **FLES** helps students develop a positive self-image as they are successful in the day-to-day language accomplishments.
- **FLES** helps students prepare for travel, work, and living outside the United States.
- **FLES** creates more interest in other languages and the people who speak them.
- **FLES** helps to create more interest in school work in general.
- **FLES** helps in the development of a firm foundation in pronunciation at an optimum time for achieving success in this skill.

- **FLES** helps in the expansion of children's horizons.
- **FLES** delivers language learning in thematic and situational packages, and has proficiency as its long-range goal.
- **FLES** helps students understand the contributions of different cultures to this country and to the world.

FLES appeals to many different people. For example, a superintendent of schools of a large school district said

> I believe that the earlier we can have youngsters come in contact with a second language, the more they will learn, the more retention they will have.

A principal of an elementary school said

> I have always been an advocate and strong supporter of having foreign languages in the elementary schools as a supplement to the curriculum. I have always felt that learning a foreign language increases the students' understanding of a country and its culture.

A parent of a fourth-grade child expressed great enthusiasm for a **FLES** program in her child's school:

> The elementary school age children have an enthusiasm to learn that will not always be with them. While learning colors, foods, and numbers, children are made aware of the customs, family lifestyles, history, art, and culture of other children in the world at a time when they need to know there are many other ways, besides their own, in which to live and work.
>
> In response to the suggestion to leave foreign languages to the high schools, it is usually too late, once they have become teenagers, to convince them that they should be interested in something else besides their school social life and career goals. It is common knowledge that older students have far more difficulty learning a second language than elementary school age children. The difficulty could be lessened quite a bit, if the student had a basic understanding and interest implanted in elementary school.
>
> Students are made to realize the importance of other ways of doing things. This may well be one of the best ways to teach the new generation not to discriminate against, belittle, or be unwilling to accept people simply because they are "foreign." If students have had no exposure to, or appreciation of, foreign languages and lifestyles, or understand that people can be different, they will have no understanding, respect, or interest in foreign concerns and people.

FLES is not, however, fun and games to the exclusion of sequential development of language skills in FLES and FLEX, or to the exclusion of content in immersion programs. When effectively taught, the learning process in **FLES** is joyful for students and teachers. This is the not-so-secret "secret" component of **FLES!**

QUESTIONS FREQUENTLY ASKED ABOUT FLES*

Why start a foreign language in elementary school?
Although much research is still needed in the various areas related to **FLES**, there are a few studies that point to the many educational benefits of introducing a foreign language in elementary school. Krashen and Terrell (95) have noted that children pick up the pronunciation very quickly, and adopt positive attitudes toward the people who speak the language. In addition, Krashen and Terrell say that from the long-range point of view, "those who start second languages as children will usually reach higher levels of competence than those who start as adults."

What is the optimum age level to introduce a foreign language?
Dr. Wilder Penfield (Penfield 163), a well-known Canadian neuropsychologist, wrote that because "the uncommitted cortex must be conditioned for speech in the first decade," the study of a foreign language is best introduced before the age of ten, in order to capitalize upon children's physical and psychological abilities. This does not mean, however, that it is not possible to begin a foreign language after the age of ten. Here, as in other instances, it depends upon the goals and expectations of the local community.

If we add an additional subject to the elementary school curriculum, such as a foreign language, can we anticipate that children will make the same progress in basic subjects such as reading and mathematics?
Over the years, there have been some objections raised to the addition of an extra subject into the elementary school curriculum that might have adverse effects upon normal educational growth patterns. Research studies such as those contributed by Lopato (126) and Rafferty (166) have shown that normal prog-

ress in basic elementary school subjects is made even with the inclusion of a foreign language in the curriculum. Similar research studies were reported by Donoghue (45). A more recent study conducted by Lipton (110) obtained similar results, as follows:

A Comparison of IOWA TESTS of Basic Skills Results for LEX* Participants and Nonparticipants

		Participants in Languages Experience Program		Nonparticipants in Languages Experience Program	
		Number	Mean	Number	Mean
Grade 3	Ability	276	110	587	106
	Vocabulary	279	4.3	587	4.1
	Reading Comprehension	279	4.5	587	4.1
	Language Total	275	5.0	587	4.6
Grade 5	Ability	349	111	308	108
	Vocabulary	347	6.1	308	5.8
	Reading Comprehension	347	6.1	308	5.8
	Language Total	348	6.6	308	6.1

LEX = FLEX

Does it cost a lot to start a FLES* program?

Cost is certainly a factor in establishing a **FLES** program, no matter which type is considered. However, since there are a number of options available in accordance with the local needs and objectives, even a minimal program with very minimal costs could be planned, provided that the goals are limited and clearly understood by everyone involved. Certainly a more sophisticated program might have a more costly budget. With immersion programs, the start-up costs are high.

Who should study a foreign language in elementary school— just gifted students?

Experience has shown that all children can learn some foreign language skills if taught with patience and effective pedagogy. This is probably most true when the objectives of the program are only for language awareness and exploratory. For more able students, a four-skills approach (listening, speaking, reading, writing) plus cultural awareness might provide a challenge to their talents and abilities. An immersion program likewise would be effective.

Does the study of a foreign language in the early years change attitudes?

Studies have shown that the early introduction of a foreign language tends to break down the "monocultural" outlook of children. This was observed to be true during the early days of **FLES** in the sixties and confirmed by the more recent research on bilingual education and immersion programs in Canada. (See Lambert and Tucker, 99.) Many of the immersion models in the U.S. are magnet programs, which achieve tremendous gains in both language proficiency and open-minded attitudes.

If a child studies a foreign language in elementary school and continues the same language, will results in high school and college show greater language proficiency?

There is a limited body of research concerning the effects of **FLES** upon later foreign language achievement. In the sixties, in the Somerville (New Jersey) schools (see 188), foreign language achievement of high school students with and without prior **FLES** study were compared. The results showed that former **FLES** students achieved scores approximately 10 percent higher than those students who had not had previous **FLES** experience. Furthermore, former **FLES** students scored, on the average, 67 points higher than non-**FLES** pupils on the C.E.E.B. Spanish and French Achievement College Board examinations.

In another study conducted in Lexington, Massachusetts (Brega and Newell, 27), results on the MLA Cooperative Foreign Language Tests indicated that those students who had had **FLES** had a more comprehensive proficiency with the language. John Carroll (31) found in studies with college students that those who had had **FLES** outperformed those who had not had **FLES**. Vocolo's study (212) obtained similar results.

While these studies took place in the 1960s, they are still valid—but obviously, much more updated longitudinal research is needed.

Is it true that children who have been exposed to a foreign language in the early years often find it easier to learn other languages throughout their lives?

Many teachers have observed this to be true, although there has been little research to confirm it. Teachers find that those students who have studied another foreign language find it much easier to adjust to a different sound and structure system.

Since the goal of learning languages is performance or proficiency, can't this be achieved in a short period of time, like commercial language schools?

It would appear that the amount of time and the quality of that time are important in helping students achieve language proficiency. Adults can accomplish this in a short time when they are highly motivated and can devote their time intensively toward language learning, particularly if they have language ability. For most people, however, effective instructional programs, as well as an early beginning, would help to ensure greater language control and achievement.

Which language(s) would be most important for elementary school children to learn?

The choice of language should be decided at the local school (county or district) level with input from the parents, as should the specific goals of the program. Some school districts even believe that it is valuable to introduce one language one year and another language the next year, but this is valid only when the goals are language awareness or exploration. Generally, it is most effective when a school district starts a **FLES** program that can articulate with the languages being taught in the junior and senior high schools. Some districts select languages of the minority groups in the community to assist in better intercultural understanding.

What is the best way to teach foreign languages in the elementary school?

Effective pedagogical procedures will be discussed in more detail in chapters 6 and 7. In general, the best approach is to teach pupils how to listen carefully, how to pronounce accurately, how to read and write limited material, and how to role-play by being in "foreign shoes." Thus, it is recommended that children in **FLES** programs be taught listening, speaking, reading, writing, and cultural skills appropriate to the goals of the program and the abilities of the students.

Who should teach foreign language in the elementary school?

This is discussed in greater detail in chapter 4. However, different types of teachers are used. Some people currently teaching are elementary school and (with additional training) secondary school teachers, foreign language specialists in **FLES**, bilingual teachers, other school personnel with language backgrounds, and volunteers, including high school and college students. The type of teacher selected for the program depends on the goals of the program and the available funds, but they should have the competencies listed in Chapter 4.

FLES* programs were widespread in the 1960s, but began to lose community support in the 1970s. Why did this happen if FLES* is such a good thing? Is it likely to happen again?

That **FLES** is "a good thing" is widely accepted by educators, administrators, parents, and others concerned with quality schools. The reasons for **FLES** failure in the 1960s are many and complex, and it is important to examine these reasons (See Chapter 4). Perhaps an oversimplification is to state that funding was the primary cause. Another basic reason was the fact that programs were exploratory in nature, yet failed to deliver the proficiency promised at that time. Also, many of the people teaching in **FLES** programs were not certified foreign language or **FLES** teachers and had not received specialized training. Still another reason was the lack of acceptance of the program in the junior and senior high schools, and a countless number of youngsters had to start their language study anew, as if they had gained nothing in the elementary school years. This problem of articulation will be discussed in greater detail in Chapter 4.

We have been hearing that immersion programs offer the best results. Is this true? Which type of program is best?

The results obtained by immersion programs are very good, but it would be unfortunate to state that this type of program is the *only* viable program for elementary schools. Many parents, for example, are still wary of having the basic skills of elementary school taught in the foreign language. However, Canadian and U.S. studies show that outstanding results in foreign language achievement can be obtained through immersion programs. Campbell *et al.* (30) and Genesee (68) indicate that immersion students achieve the highest proficiency levels of the three types of **FLES** programs. Some educators and parents think that this type of program is not for all students. There is no "best" type of program, as each program selected should be tailor-made to the needs of the students, the school, and the community, based on the goals established for the program. In some instances, the "best" program will be a sequential FLES program. In others, it will be an immersion program. In still others it will be a language-awareness **FLES** program. The "best" type of program is one that states its objectives and then is able to deliver the program delineated by these objectives.

Why do researchers indicate that it is better to begin a foreign language when a child is young, before puberty?

Second language experts Dulay, Burt, and Krashen (50) have stated that

> children appear to be much more successful than adults in acquiring the phonological system of the new language; many eventually attain native-like accents. . . . Most children are ultimately more successful than adults in learning a second language, but they are not always faster.

They feel that there are several reasons for this: biological timetable, cognitive factors, affective factors, and differences in the language environment. Fathman (57) concurs. There has been considerable research on these factors in the bilingual schools of Canada, and a growing body of evidence from successful programs in the United States.

Are there more supporters of early foreign language today than in the past twenty years?

More educators and parents seem to feel that starting children in some form of foreign language study in the grades is significant in quality education. For example, an organization of southern governors recommended that "foreign language education be made available to children as early as the first grade," because they found that a lack of knowledge of a foreign language was a factor in this country's international ignorance, as reported by Vobejda (211).

A former U.S. Ambassador to Japan, Edwin O. Reischauer, is quoted in Paul Simon's book, *The Tongue-Tied American* (185): "foreign language instruction should come early in the educational process, basically at the elementary level. This is because it can serve as a fundamental shaper of the child's perception of the world. . . . It should come early also because the young child learns a foreign language with ease and pleasure." Paul Simon, in support of early foreign language, also wrote that "students who have had foreign language exposure are more likely to take a language in high school than students without this background."

Another endorsement of early instruction in foreign languages appears in a publication of the U.S. Department of Education, *What Works* (217): "the best way to learn a foreign language in school is to start early and to study it intensively over many years."

Should all FLES* programs offer a long sequence in elementary school and continue in the secondary school?

A long sequence can contribute greatly to greater language proficiency. However, different districts may have different goals and certainly different budgets. The goals of the school district determine the length of the program. As long as the objectives have been clearly stated and understood by all people concerned, the length of program can be tailored to meet these goals and fit the budgetary constraints.

Why bother teaching a foreign language in elementary school for only a year or two?

It is true that a longer period of time would be more worthwhile. However, if the goals the school district can afford and wishes to implement are limited, then even a short exposure to FLEX as an introductory "taste" of foreign language will have beneficial results.

With all the subjects studied in the elementary school curriculum, isn't foreign language something that doesn't fit this curriculum?

The study of a foreign language fits very well in the elementary school curriculum. Children are naturally curious about codes and different languages. They are also very interested in different people's customs (they study some of these in social studies, don't they?). They can sing songs from other countries in the foreign language (to enrich their music program); they can perform folk dances to add an international flavor to their physical education program. They can learn about famous mathematicians and scientists from other countries. They can learn about famous artists, composers, etc., from other countries. The study of a foreign language adds a broad new dimension to the elementary school curriculum.

Do many children drop out of immersion programs because they are too demanding?

There are no statistics, as yet, on the number of dropouts from immersion programs, although some children get fatigued during the first year or so because of the challenge of the foreign language. As a matter of fact, there are no statistics on the number of dropouts in sequential FLES and FLEX programs. We do know, however, that if the methods remain the same over a number of years, the children get tired and bored with studying a foreign language.

If a school district has limited funds and wishes to select one type of program, which program would it be and in which grade level should it begin?

This is a question that has to be studied at the school district level, following some of the suggestions in Chapter 4. It cannot be answered in general terms, because the needs of each school district are different. Perhaps one general answer is, try to work backwards from the starting point in the secondary schools. For example, if the secondary school program begins in grade 7, then a grade 6 **FLES** program might be started the first year, grades 5 and 6 in the second year, and grades 4, 5, and 6 in the third year, and so on.

If immersion programs get the highest level of proficiency, why shouldn't all FLES* programs be immersion programs?

It is true that immersion programs get the best results in language proficiency. But since both qualified teachers and materials are difficult to obtain (see Anderson and Rhodes, 6), immersion programs may be difficult to implement and maintain. Here again, the program type selected *must* match the goals selected by the school community.

Is grammar taught in FLES* programs? How can children learn the language without learning grammar?

Grammar as such is not formally taught in **FLES** programs. Children are, however, exposed to correct forms and usage in the foreign language, and they tend to use the language functionally, as they have heard it. That is why a teacher highly proficient in the foreign language is essential in all types of **FLES** programs. Although the youngsters cannot quote the grammar rules, they learn how to use the language correctly in functional situations. Furthermore, if students request specific grammar information, explanations are given in accordance with their ability to comprehend.

More details about these questions and others will be developed in later chapters of this book.

HIGHLIGHTS

- **There is no *one* best program type**
- **There are many reasons to develop FLES* programs**
- **FLES* is gaining many supporters**
- **More research studies support early language learning**

III

Goals and Objectives

Before embarking on the establishment of one specific type of **FLES** program, it is important (and necessary) for the various persons responsible for making decisions to raise a number of questions and try to get some answers from the group and from "experts" outside the group.

It is the goal of this section to serve as a guide for planning committees considering the options for their schools. For each program type, a number of questions is indicated. These questions ideally will trigger in the planning group additional questions that may be pertinent to the local needs.

GENERAL CONSIDERATIONS

Students: Which students will receive the instruction? Which grade(s)?

Goals: Are they limited? Exactly what is expected by parents, administrators, and members of the community?

Teachers: Are teachers readily available? Are they qualified?

Long-range plans: How will the program fit into these plans?

Finances: Is there money for teachers and materials, or is the funding very limited? What are the sources of the funding? Is the funding for one year only or more?

Content: Will it be possible to develop an appropriate curriculum? Who will do this? Will it cover only one year? Is there a plan for dovetailing the curriculum with the secondary school curriculum?

Status in the elementary school: Does foreign language study have an important identity in the overall elementary school plan? Is it before, during, or after school? How does it fit into the rest of the elementary school curriculum?

Evaluation: How will it be determined whether the goals of the program have been met in its language and cultural accomplishments? (For immersion students, have they covered the elementary school curriculum?)

Materials: Are materials available for the type of program desired? Are they available for the first year? For more than one year? Are they varied? Are they appropriate for elementary school youngsters? Are they culturally authentic?

Time: What kind of time is available? Is this sufficient to accomplish the established goals? Is it the same each year? How long for each session? How many times a week? What has to be left out of the school schedule?

Coordination: Is someone going to be able to coordinate all the facets of the program? Is it someone who is knowledgeable about **FLES**? Is it someone who understands foreign languages?

Language: Which language is going to meet the needs of the students best? Which language can be continued at the secondary school level? Is it important to continue it? Would it be better to start a language that requires a greater amount of time to learn, such as Russian or Japanese?

Resources: Have all the resources in the community been identified? Which people, inside and outside the school system, can be of help? Which businesses in the community could assist the program? Which governmental agencies could encourage the program? Which international agencies (such as embassies) are available for materials and services? Which universities could offer support services?

Thus, in many ways, the questions to be asked and answered are similar for sequential FLES, FLEX, and immersion models. After securing answers to these general questions, a planning committee might then examine the various models.

FOR THE FLEX PROGRAM MODEL

- Would it be possible to offer the foreign language to all students? Is any funding available? Is it "hidden"? (i.e., can existing funding cover some aspects?)
- What are the specific language and cultural goals? Would the limited results warrant the expenditure of time and money? How much proficiency is expected?
- Are the goals doable? Will the goals be clearly stated?
- Is it important to hire only qualified teachers?
- Should the program be devoted to only one language, or would it be possible to provide exposure to more than one language and culture?
- Is it possible for elementary school teachers to teach FLEX, using cassettes, video, and film?
- Who will be responsible for the program, districtwide and in the school(s)?
- Can the program be initiated even when there is little money for materials and curriculum development?
- Can the program be started with only 15 minutes available a week? Should it be?
- How can the FLEX program model be evaluated? By questionnaires, examinations, interviews, etc.?
- How would this FLEX program compare with other FLEX program models in the country?

FOR THE FLES PROGRAM MODEL

- Would it be possible to offer the foreign language to all students? The first year only? How much funding is available?

- What are the specific language and cultural goals? Are these in keeping with the needs of the community?
- Are the goals attainable? Are they appropriate? Clearly stated?
- Who would be qualified to teach in this program?
- Which language will be selected? What is the rationale for the selection of this language? Is this in keeping with the needs and wishes of the community?
- Which materials would be appropriate for this type of program? Audio, video, film, television, etc.? Are textbooks available? For one year or for more than one year? Are they culturally authentic?
- Who will be responsible for the program, districtwide and in the school(s)? Someone who knows foreign languages and FLES?
- Should the program be initiated without adequate materials and curriculum development?
- What is the minimum amount of time needed to achieve the established goals for this program? How will the time be found?
- How can the FLES program model be evaluated? By questionnaires, examinations, interviews, skills testing and other ways?
- How would this FLES program compare with other FLES program models in the country?
- How would this FLES program compare with a FLEX or an immersion program model in meeting the established goals?

FOR THE IMMERSION MODEL (ALSO PARTIAL IMMERSION)

- Would it be possible for all students to be in the immersion model? The first year only? Partial immersion? For only some of the students? How much funding is there?
- What are the specific goals? Do they include language and cultural goals as well as basic subject goals? Are these in keeping with the needs of the community?
- Are the goals doable, realistic?

- Who would be qualified to teach in this program? Are there enough qualified teachers for this program model?

- Which language will be selected? What is the rationale for the selection of this language? When will English start? Does the language choice meet the needs of the community?

- How do parents feel about the immersion model? Are there special concerns about progress in the curriculum and English?

- Which materials would be appropriate for this type of model? Are there sufficient materials available not only in language, but in the language for math, science, social studies? Are they all foreign materials? Would they be appropriate for the curriculum?

- Who will be responsible for the program, districtwide and in the school(s)? What will occur in the junior high school for these immersion students? Will there be an immersion junior high school?

- Who will develop the curriculum in the several areas of immersion? Will they be translations of the English? Is this satisfactory?

- Will it be total immersion or partial immersion to achieve the goals of the program?

- How can the immersion program model be evaluated?

- How would this immersion program compare with other immersion program models in the country?

- How would this immersion program compare with a FLES program or a FLEX program in meeting the established goals of this school community?

THE GOAL-SETTING PROCESS

In answering the questions listed above (and others), it is essential to note that setting the goals and objectives is paramount to the success of any contemplated program. These will determine the answers for all the other components, and these goals are the ones established for the implementation and evaluation of the program model selected.

After a choice has been made, based on the program goals and objectives, it is important to include a flexibility component in the program model so that changes can be made when the program is not fulfilling the goals.

If flexibility is considered to be an ongoing factor, the beginning grade level can be changed (e.g., changing the beginning grade level from grade 4 to grade 3), adjusting the content of the curriculum if it turns out to be too demanding for the time allotted to the program, and addressing other developmental concerns. However, if a major change seems to be indicated (such as a change from a sequential FLES program model to a FLEX program model, or from an immersion model to a FLEX model), it is essential that a broadly based committee be involved in studying the reasons for making such a change. I would urge that no major changes be made for at least two years before a study committee begins to look into other options. If the original study committee followed the 21 steps outlined in Chapter 4, a *major* change would probably be unnecessary.

Probably the most significant goal to be determined is the one concerning the degree of proficiency to be attained. In making this determination, it is basic that any committee involved in the planning consult with **FLES** language specialists to make certain that the committee's expectations are realistic and in keeping with what is already known about second language instruction. As Met (142) observed, "FLES, FLEX, and immersion are all effective approaches to language and culture study for children. . . . [I]t is important to understand that the kind of program selected will result in different proficiency levels."

In making a decision, a school community committee needs to ask itself various questions like: "How much language proficiency do we want? "What do we want the children to be able to do?" "How much cultural awareness do we want?" "Are there other factors in the community that might impel us to select one language over another, particularly if there are people in the community representative of language minorities?" and other questions. If a very high level of proficiency is required, then the immersion model or even partial immersion can produce such results. If the primary goal of the elementary school language program is cultural awareness with varying degrees of language proficiency, then either the sequential FLES or the FLEX model can offer viable results. Other variations within each major model can be arranged, from an itinerant specialist teacher in **FLES** programs to non–foreign language specialist classroom teachers in the FLEX model. Still others include the use of television and satellite programs, combined with both types of teachers. Still others involve the use of volunteers, where funding proves to be a problem. But in each case, the goals and objectives must be spelled out completely, so that no one is misled. That is central!

For additional information on goals, see the Bibliography: Lipton *et al.*, 109; Rhodes and Schreibstein, 169; and Schinko-Llano, 178.

HIGHLIGHTS

- **Long-range goals must be spelled out in advance**

- **There must be realistic, attainable goals, understood and accepted by key people**

- **The type of program selected is determined by the goals**

IV

How to Organize Programs

THE TWENTY-ONE STEPS

The following twenty-one steps may be of help to communities attempting to organize **FLES** programs:

1. Assess community/school interests and needs
2. Organize an advisory or study committee
3. Determine the resources of the school and the community with respect to finances, language preferences, secondary school programs, agencies, universities, etc.
4. Formulate realistic goals for the community (long-range plans have to be made concerning curriculum and articulation)
5. Anticipate difficulties, problems, roadblocks, and views of people who might be opposed
6. Investigate successful programs; discuss possible problems
7. Contact knowledgeable people, particularly second-language specialists in the different types of **FLES** programs
8. Prepare a detailed proposal including a plan for a pilot program, with anticipated budget and outcomes of the program selected
9. Arrange for coordination of the program
10. Develop curriculum materials to fulfill the realistic goals, as well as plans for articulation with upper levels

11. Develop a plan for the recruitment and selection of teachers

12. Develop a plan for teacher training (preservice and inservice)

13. Promote interest by speaking to parents, teachers, principals, civic association members, etc.

14. Be sure to involve secondary school foreign language teachers in the study committee

15. Order materials of instruction

16. Arrange teaching schedules

17. Begin the program and *publicize the program!*

18. Evaluate! Evaluate! Evaluate! Ask for input at all levels and at all stages of planning and implementation

19. Be prepared for successes and failures

20. Attempt to solve conflicts and unexpected reactions

21. After a year's pilot and possibly another year of trial and error making necessary modifications, be prepared to enjoy the program!

These twenty-one steps are certainly an oversimplification of a long and arduous process (possibly 9 to 18 months) of implementing a new program. However, no matter which model is selected, a school district needs to touch all or most of these steps in the organization of a foreign language program in the elementary school.

Assessment of interest and need should come first, and probably has to be ongoing, even after an advisory or study committee has been organized. Before embarking on any change, the Superintendent and his/her staff would want to see if there is some base of support in the community.

The study committee should be composed of foreign language educators representing all school levels, parents, taxpayers, administrators, business representatives, guidance counselors, and specialists in elementary education—including some representation from the university level—and others according to local requirements. The committee could then divide the work in order to obtain answers to the various questions raised. They might visit other programs, gather significant information and send questionnaires, hire consultants, hold hearings, and, finally, make recommendations on the essential components of the **FLES** proposal, which *should* include information about the following (including a rationale for each):

- Program design and goals
- Selection (if any) of students
- Grade level(s)
- Selection of language(s)
- Coordination and supervision
- Articulation
- Schedule of classes
- Selection of foreign language teachers
- Training of foreign language teachers
- Role of the classroom teacher
- Budget estimation, source(s) of funding, length of funding
- Content of instruction
- Methodology
- Materials of instruction
- Scheduling
- Examination of existing elementary school schedule to determine how foreign language will fit in
- Determination of what will be left out of the elementary school schedule
- Summary of research
- Review of other programs
- If immersion, which subjects to be taught in the FL?
- If immersion, when will English be started? Who will teach it?
- Procedures for evaluation of pilot program
- Ongoing procedures for evaluation of the program
- Other pertinent data relating to the local situation
- Development of plans for publicizing the program

For additional information about the options in making these decisions, see the Bibliography: Gradisnik 72; Gramer, 73; Lipton *et al.*, 109; and Met, 142.

CAUTIONS!

At the height of enthusiasm for a new fad, policymakers and study committees may tend *not* to consider some of the problems and negative aspects of a project.

I must stress that before a community embarks on instituting any type of **FLES** program, it should consider *all* the implications for the next 3 to 5 years and beyond. It does not make any sense to introduce a **FLES** program for one year, only to disband it the next year. That is why both short- and long-range goals have to be discussed, modified, changed, adapted, and developed until they represent the best thinking of the community. "What if" suppositions should be posed throughout the planning process. "Why" questions should be asked throughout the planning process. "Are we better off with the program or without the program?" should be asked throughout the planning process. Careful consideration of many options will ensure an effective program, based on long- and short-range planning.

The seesaw phenomenon of "Hooray for **FLES**" and "Down with **FLES**" need not be repeated if we analyze some of the difficulties that occurred with **FLES** programs during the 1960s and 1970s.

HOW TO AVOID THE DISASTERS OF THE SIXTIES (OR—FOLLOW THIS BLUEPRINT OF WHAT HAPPENED!)

It is my opinion (and that of many others) that **FLES** programs of the sixties and seventies failed for many reasons:

1. **FLES** programs grew too rapidly, without too much careful thought and planning beyond the first year.
2. **FLES** programs made promises and set goals that were often unattainable, given the amount of time for instruction and the lack of qualified teachers.
3. **FLES** programs failed because they did not have the support of secondary school teachers and supervisors.
4. The rationale for starting a **FLES** program then was more often based on a "bandwagon phenomenon" than on a sound and thoughtful examination of resources and goals.

5. While it is true that funding became a crucial factor in whether a **FLES** program continued, taxpayers demanded (and rightly so) to know how their tax money was being spent, and whether this was the most efficient way to spend the money. In other words, were the results what they had been promised?

6. At that time, very little attention was given to flexibility, since language teaching relied heavily on pattern drills and behavioral objectives. The then new audiolingual methodology, with its heavy reliance on pattern drills for listening and speaking activities, swept the country on all school levels. Authorities proclaimed that a prereading and writing stage should be included at all levels, and for **FLES**, a minimum of 100 clock hours of solely listening and speaking activities was required. This amounted to at least one year for most **FLES** programs. Hopefully, what we have learned from the failure of some programs of the sixties will prevent us from falling into a "regimentation" trap. In the sixties, the "methodology" was used for all kinds of programs. Now we know that we must suit both the program type and the methodology to the goals of the program, no matter what the methodology fashion of the times may be. Now we know that we must be flexible and realistic in approach, in both planning and implementation.

7. Not many **FLES** programs at that time had qualified teachers, as opportunities for preservice and inservice were very limited. Some programs relied heavily on native speakers with little training in elementary schools in the U.S. and little exposure to second-language teaching methodology.

8. The long sequence of studying a foreign language with very little change in methodology resulted in some youngsters getting tired of and bored with studying a foreign language.

9. Articulation with the secondary schools was almost nonexistent, and former **FLES** students entering secondary school programs found that they had to begin the language from the beginning. This was frustrating for students and parents.

10. Since **FLES** at that time was mostly listening and speaking, with very little reading and writing, and relying mostly on songs and games, it was not taken seriously, even though most of the children learned both language and culture.

Even today, some adults who are former **FLES** students still remember their foreign language experience with great fondness in their interviews with me!

11. At that time it was considered essential to form a "cultural island," quite apart from the rest of the elementary school curriculum. This exclusivity made it easier to remove such a program than one involved with the rest of the curriculum activities.

12. **FLES** was started in the sixties as a reaction to the surprise of Sputnik. Sputnik, readers may recall, was the first earth satellite launched by the Russians in 1957. As a result, policy makers across the nation insisted that science, mathematics, and foreign languages be expanded and supported at all levels. Federal language institutes were funded, and foreign language teachers were exposed to the new wave of audiolingual methodology, which promised more effective results in language learning on all school levels, including the **FLES** level. It was felt that in order for our children to be able to learn a difficult language such as Russian, they needed a long time. By the seventies, the pressure for early language learning diminished and technological advancement became the object of public lobbying.

Can similar failures be avoided? Of course! With the involvement of a number of key people (both professional and community leaders) with a long-range public commitment, with careful setting of realistic goals within the framework of available monies, teachers, content, time schedules, and other factors, it *is* possible to plan successful programs for the eighties and beyond.

COORDINATION OF THE PROGRAM

Included in any plan for developing a **FLES** program must be a decision on who will coordinate it. Whether it is coordinated by a teacher, a supervisor, an administrator, a chairperson, a parent, there must be someone who makes the decisions, who answers the questions and complaints (yes, once in a while there are some complaints!), who assists with hiring and firing staff, who orders materials, and who is in overall charge of the program. This person is the **FLES** advocate. Even with the most enlightened philosophy of management, there must be one person who has the final word.

Experience reminds us that the best person for this role is a foreign language supervisor, who sees the program in the entire sweep of a K–12 program. However, sometimes it is necessary for a non-foreign language administrator to head the program. It is incumbent upon this person to become as knowledgeable as possible and to seek counsel from other foreign language people before making any major decisions.

In planning a projected budget, school districts should keep in mind that they must budget a position for a coordinator. The program cannot run effectively without leadership, and this position must be planned in advance or dovetailed with another, similar position. If the district elects to save money and combine **FLES** with another existing position, extreme care must be taken so as not to overburden any one individual. Coordination of the program will take time: there must be time to arrange for teacher training and inservice; there must be time to meet with parents, administrators, principals; there must be time to develop curriculum; there must be time to observe the program; there must be time to think of additional ways to make the program even more effective; there must be time to make long-range plans and get consensus on them. Coordination is essential!

For additional suggestions on coordination of programs, see the Bibliography: Donoghue and Kunkle, 46; Donoghue, 48; Finocchiaro, 59; Lipton and Mirsky, 116; Lipton and Alkonis, 122; MacRae, 130; Sims and Hammond, 186.

THE ROLE OF PARENTS

Parents can be helpful in supporting all types of **FLES** programs. They can do this in the following ways:

- Help the child see foreign words in newspapers and magazines or on labels on different products
- Purchase books and records on the child's level, although this is primarily for enrichment
- Encourage the child who may feel discouraged or stressed (in immersion programs)

- Keep in touch with the child's teacher to learn how they can help
- Assist the teacher by going on trips related to the foreign language work
- Talk to the class about their experiences in the foreign culture
- Speak to the class in the foreign language
- Speak to the class about their work in the foreign culture and opportunities for careers with foreign language backgrounds
- Encourage but not force the child to speak the foreign language at home
- Make sure that they let the child know that they are happy about the child's progress
- Serve on an Advisory Board for the school
- Speak about positive and negative aspects with parents of children who may be contemplating entrance into the foreign language program
- Confer with the principal on various aspects of the program that may need rethinking
- Try to give the child opportunities for participating in some aspect of the foreign culture at museums, on trips, on television programs, etc.
- Try to keep the entire program in perspective while resolving day-to-day concerns

For additional suggestions on parental involvement in **FLES** programs, see the Bibliography: Andersson, 8; Bellevue, 22; Ehrlich, 54; and Harding and Riley, 78.

PLANNING FOR THE CURRICULUM

The curriculum must suit the program and the goals selected. Consideration must be given to content, the skills (listening, speaking, reading, writing) to be emphasized, the amount of English (if any) to be used, the instructional approach, the link between the foreign language and other aspects of the elementary school curriculum, the development of an initial program and plans for its continuation, the thorny problem of what to do with the youngster who moves into the community without any foreign language experience, the guest speakers who would enhance the curriculum, and finally, whether students' **FLES** experience will be ignored or will be incorporated into the middle school and/or junior high school program. (This will be discussed in greater detail in the section "Articulation.")

It is difficult to make decisions about curriculum if the long-range goals are not firmly in place. If a program had been in existence in grade 7, for example, and the new elementary school program has been planned to be phased in each year, first in grade 6, next year in grade 5, and so, it is essential to view the effect of the elementary school program on the secondary school program. If, on the other hand, a new FLEX program is exploratory in nature, and no one expects students to build on the early introduction, that is quite a different story. If this were the case, the limited goals and exploratory nature of the program would be understood and accepted by parents, teachers, and administrators. Usually when a new **FLES** program is developed and implemented, plans have to be made for the revision of the secondary school program, particularly if a great number of students are involved.

Thus, when first planning a new program, the study committee must deal with the reality of the kind of program it will be, what the expected outcomes will be, and how this type of program fits into the short- and long-range educational sequence from the curriculum point of view. If a revision of the secondary school curriculum will be required, that revision should be started long before the new **FLES** students arrive at the secondary school. Long-range planning is a *must!*

If the study committee recommends an immersion program, then long-range plans should be put in operation immediately, so that immersion students can continue their program in an immersion component at the middle/junior high school and even the high school. Long-range curriculum planning must look ahead five to ten years, anticipating problems and putting down the framework for an effective articulation plan.

For a further discussion of curriculum, please see Chapter 5.

ARTICULATION

The question of articulation is one of the most difficult problems when dealing with sequential FLES or immersion. In FLEX programs the situation is much simpler—most parents and students do not expect to continue the foreign language in the secondary school program. But even with FLEX, it is disappointing when children who have had a brief introduction to a foreign language are required to start from the very beginning. What a turnoff! Yet, from the point of view of the secondary school, when there are a handful of youngsters who have had exposure to a foreign language, scheduling complexities prevent keeping all students in the same class so as to provide continuity of learning.

After three years or more of sequential FLES or immersion, when students with a rather strong background in the foreign language have to start all over again or decide to drop the foreign language studied and opt for a completely new foreign language, the disappointment for students and their parents is even greater. There are few simple answers to the problem. However, here are a few suggestions:

- Former FLES or immersion students can be encouraged to work on the next stages of learning on an independent study basis.

- Such students may be offered one class at the senior high school in order to continue on their proper level.

- Such students may be offered a maintenance class that will help them retain their language skills; they may move ahead when they enter high school.

- District plans that develop an elementary school immersion program should also include plans for an immersion junior and senior high school if at all possible.

For additional suggestions on articulation, see the Bibliography: Andersson, 9; Larew, 102; and Lipton et al., 109.

RECRUITMENT AND SELECTION OF TEACHERS

Fluency or proficiency in the foreign language to be taught is the basic requirement of the would-be FLES/FLEX/

immersion teacher. Since young children imitate almost everything they hear, it is extremely important for teachers of this level to provide a model for the youngsters. Thus, ability in the foreign language is of great importance to the success of the program. Part of the interview for prospective teachers should be conducted in the foreign language. Furthermore, not only oral skills are needed, but written skills are important, too.

Interviews

Other questions that might be discussed at an interview are the following:

1. How would you begin a **FLES** program? What would you do the first week?
2. What are your goals for the first year? the second year? etc.
3. How would you teach a dialogue, a narrative, drills of various kinds?
4. How would you provide for individual differences and different learning styles?
5. How would you handle the disruptive pupil? the child who doesn't respond? the student who is bored?
6. How would you keep all the children interested? motivated to learn?
7. How would you evaluate pupil achievement in the foreign language?
8. How would you evaluate your effectiveness as a teacher?
9. How and when would you introduce reading and writing skills?
10. What kinds of audiovisual equipment would you use?
11. How would the rest of the elementary school program bear on what you teach in the foreign language?
12. What would be your relationship with the classroom teacher, the principal, and the parents?
13. What would you do if the children did not understand the foreign language?
14. How would you create a classroom climate for effective learning?

15. How would you help the children to be relaxed and reduce their anxiety levels?

Although there are no correct or incorrect answers for these suggested interview questions, nor are they meant to be exhaustive, it is possible, through questioning, to determine the candidate's philosophy of teaching, enthusiasm, understanding of the youngster in elementary and middle schools, and training in methodology for teaching foreign languages to young students.

Screening

Each local agency would probably wish to develop its own requirements, since few states, at the present time, have statewide requirements—although a few states are currently developing guidelines. As a guide for school communities, the following criteria might be useful for initial screening of applicants:

- Proficiency in the foreign language to be taught (in all four skills—listening, speaking, reading, and writing)
- Proficiency in another foreign language (optional)
- Knowledge of the customs and culture of the people who speak the foreign language
- Knowledge of the nature of the elementary and/or middle school youngster and the elementary school program
- Knowledge of the content of FLES/FLEX/immersion programs
- Knowledge of the pedagogy for teaching foreign language to young students
- Knowledge of the methodology for teaching reading skills
- Ability to plan interesting and challenging lessons
- Ability to use a variety of materials
- Ability to relate to people of all ages
- Ability to be a "team player" on the educational team
- Ability to enjoy working with young students
- Ability to teach, as evidenced by an approved form of student teaching experience

It should be noted that it is easier to staff FLES and FLEX programs because there are, at present, few candidates for immersion who are highly proficient in two languages (English and the foreign language). It is generally expected that the immersion teacher will be responsible for the content teaching in the foreign language and the teaching of English, although some programs have a different teacher responsible for teaching English. Based on my experience, I do not see any real need to insist on this procedure, since a bilingual teacher could serve as a role model for the students in the immersion program. Others say that students would use more English if they knew that they could speak to their teachers in English. I do not agree. While children might, at first, test the situation, they would soon recognize that English has a definite time and place, no matter who is teaching it. It is also difficult to find prospective candidates with these demanding foreign language skills who are also familiar with American elementary school procedures and practices. Just hiring a native speaker without these additional skills is not a good practice.

Competencies

Which competencies should be expected of prospective FLES, FLEX, and immersion teachers? The following competencies might provide some insight into the range of abilities required for a successful foreign language teacher at the elementary school level:

Language proficiency in the foreign language

Listening skills: able to understand the foreign language as spoken by a native at a normal conversational tempo

Speaking skills: able to speak the foreign language with sufficient command to communicate spontaneously on daily-life topics with a native speaker without major syntactic errors

Reading skills: able to read foreign language materials of a general nature with immediate comprehension (such materials as newspapers, magazines, etc.)

Writing skills: able to write foreign language material (letters, reports, summaries, etc.) with minimal errors, and have some knowledge of stylistics to express the subtleties of the language

Language proficiency in English

The competencies for this category would be the same as those listed for the foreign language category.

Some would disagree with the notion that English proficiency is essential in the teaching of FLES, FLEX, and immersion. Based on my experience I find that a teacher who herself/himself has understood what it means to study a foreign language will be more empathetic to the students. Also, the teacher who is thoroughly familiar with both languages will be in a better position to understand and anticipate the language problems of her/his students.

Linguistics

Knowledge of the principles of phonology, morphology, and syntax, and the ability to apply these principles to strategies for second language instruction.

Methodology for FLES and FLEX

- Effective techniques for classroom management
- Unit, weekly, daily lesson planning
- Strategies for teaching the four skills (listening, speaking, reading, and writing) and culture
- Techniques for working with groups
- Error correction techniques
- Evaluation techniques
- Procedures for teaching different types of learners
- Reinforcement and review techniques
- Current trends in second-language learning and research studies

- Effective cross-cultural strategies
- Ways to create an effective classroom climate
- Procedures for adapting texts and other materials
- Techniques for appropriate use of multimedia equipment
- Procedures for developing specific goals within the overall goals of the program
- A variety of skills, techniques, and procedures to provide a wide range of different activities in the classroom

Methodology for immersion

- Effective techniques for classroom management
- Procedures for delivering content-based instruction in the foreign language in some or all of the subjects of the elementary school curriculum
- Techniques for working in groups
- Evaluation techniques
- Procedures for teaching different types of learners
- Reinforcement and review techniques
- Current trends in immersion and research studies
- Ways to create an effective classroom climate
- Procedures for adapting texts and other materials
- Techniques for appropriate use of multimedia materials
- Procedures for developing specific goals within the overall goals of the immersion program and the elementary school program
- A variety of skills, techniques, and procedures to provide a wide range of activities in the classroom

American and target language children's literature

- Children's classics
- Fables and fairy tales
- Children's poetry

- Children's magazines and other contemporary materials
- Other literary materials appropriate to the goals of the program

Culture

The candidate should demonstrate a knowledge of, a sensitivity to, and an ability to contrast differences and similarities between the target culture and the American culture in

- Family life
- Social groups
- Political activities
- Kinesics
- Influence of the media
- Role of women
- Attitude toward money, land, food, humor, and other values
- Occupations
- Leisure-time activities, such as sports, etc.
- Geography and history
- Social, education, and governmental institutions
- Music, art, theater, cinema
- Religion
- Cuisine
- Ceremonies, customs, and rituals
- Taboos
- Science and technology
- Other aspects as needed

Child psychology

- Understanding of the nature of the elementary school child
- Knowledge of how to work successfully with children, parents, other professionals (teachers, administrators, principals, guidance counselors, psychologists, etc.)

- Knowledge of the physical, cognitive, intellectual, emotional, and social stages of elementary school growth and development
- Knowledge of the different theories of learning
- Awareness of the different ways of increasing student motivation and attention span
- Awareness of the importance of the teacher's personality in creating a warm, friendly learning environment
- Ability to plan interesting and challenging lessons that will appeal to young children
- Demonstrated ability to teach the foreign language to young children through an approved form of student teaching
- Demonstrated success in developing rapport with young children

For further information about teacher selection and teacher competencies, see the Bibliography: Hawley and Oates, 79; Koster, 92; Larew, 102; Moskowitz, 147; Notes, 150; Stewart, 202; and Wing, 220.

Volunteers

When a school system determines that it is interested in a language awareness program, or FLEX, but it cannot find the funds to deliver such a program, sometimes it is feasible to use volunteers (adults or high school and college students). In this case, it is again extremely important that the goals and expectations of such a program are clearly understood by everyone concerned, lest there be great disappointment at the minimal progress that students in such a program make. In dealing with high school students, for example, it is recommended that a contract be signed by the student, the foreign language teacher at the high school who is responsible for the training, and the elementary school principal, to include such topics as school rules, attendance and punctuality, planning, schedule, supplies, and other pertinent procedural information. (See section on the use of peer tutors in this chapter.)

Certification

Although most states and school districts do not, as yet, have certification of foreign language teachers at the elementary school level, teachers must be certified in some area. Usually, it is best to have a certified elementary school teacher with high proficiency in the foreign language. Unfortunately, there are still very few teachers with this type of background. Another alternative is to use certified foreign language teachers who are highly proficient in the foreign language and who have taken at least nine credits in elementary school methodology and curriculum, as well as a **FLES** methods course. These, too, are quite rare, but the number of qualified teachers, it is predicted, will grow, once the need is identified and announced. Immersion teachers who are totally bilingual in English and the target language are also very hard to find, but here too, as more elementary foreign language programs are expanded, more teachers will seek the appropriate training to develop the required competencies. If there is a demand for training courses, more universities will respond to this demand. As Larew (103) pointed out, the **FLES** teacher is "not merely a language teacher, but is often perceived as a representative of the culture of the language she teaches, by her students." Having proficiency in the language is excellent, but many skills and competencies are required in order to perform effectively on the **FLES** level. As Stewart (202) forcefully indicated, no teacher (implication being, a secondary school teacher) should accept an assignment on the **FLES** level without training in the specific skills demanded by the goals of the program.

At this writing, there are still very few universities and colleges that offer **FLES** methodology courses, despite the fact that there is some form of mandated program in such states as New York, Louisiana, North Carolina, and Hawaii. Besides the University of Maryland (Baltimore County) courses are offered at Bank Street College in New York City and Concordia College in Minnesota, and others from time to time.

For further information about **FLES** teacher training, see the Bibliography: Wing, 220.

OPTIONS IN STAFFING FLES* PROGRAMS

It should be pointed out that creative decisions should and could be arrived at in attempting to staff the type of **FLES** program that best suits the needs of the school and the community:

- Classroom teacher with foreign language training teaches her/his own class
- Exchange of classes: one teacher teaches the foreign language while the other teacher covers a curriculum area such as spelling, math, science, etc.
- Cluster specialist: the foreign language is taught by a specialist who also teaches other curriculum areas such as physical education, etc.
- Itinerant **FLES** teacher covering a number of classes in a number of schools
- Resource people in the schools with a strong knowledge of a foreign language:

Principal	Media Specialist
Assistant Principal	Aides
Counselors	Speech teacher
Secretaries	Others
Parents	

- Resource people outside the school:

  College students
  High school students (sometimes called cross-age tutors)
  Members of the community
  College teachers
  Part-time high school teachers
- Television programs on educational or cable TV (can be interactive)
- Supplementary audiovisual materials:

  Listening corners in the classroom
  Language masters for individual and small group practice
  Tapes
  Tapes plus written page directions
  Tapes plus transparencies

Videotapes
Sound/filmstrips
Films
Videodiscs
Computers

THE FOREIGN LANGUAGE SPECIALIST AND THE CLASSROOM TEACHER

When a foreign language specialist is responsible for teaching the foreign language, it would be helpful if the specialist enlists the aid of the classroom teacher. Sometimes this can be accomplished in a number of ways. A form of team teaching can be developed, with mutual professional respect. The foreign language specialist can provide foreign language instruction in a close working relationship with the classroom teacher, and may also assist with special foreign language events, the preparation of an assembly program, and other related events, keeping in mind, of course, that the classroom teacher is responsible for the class. The classroom teacher is encouraged to provide support for the foreign language instruction in the following ways:

- Present a positive attitude toward the foreign language learning
- Prepare the youngsters for the instruction
- Watch for topics or activities during the language lesson that can be used in follow-up activities, such as (1) playing a recording for further practice, (2) discussing an aspect of the foreign culture that may relate to a reading passage or social studies, (3) contrasting English language words and foreign language words, (4) discussing contributions of foreign words to the English language
- Encourage students to explore the language and culture in greater depth
- Plan for ways to correlate the foreign language and culture with other subjects in the elementary school curriculum
- Encourage youngsters to bring in foreign language books from the library
- Have students look for foreign words that have become a part

of the English language (e.g., *sombrero, chapeau*) in newspapers and magazines
- Have a bulletin board devoted to topics related to the foreign country or countries (current events, pictures, labels, advertisements, greeting cards)

USE OF PEER TUTORS IN A FLEX PROGRAM

Because of budgetary constraints, it is frequently possible to organize a program with cross-age tutors (students from the local high schools or colleges). Care should be taken in the selection of these peer "teachers," and particular attention should be given to their training. They should agree to some kind of contract so that they will understand their responsibilities and the elementary school will understand its responsibilities. See the sample contract on page 56. While this procedure is not generally recommended unless there are limited goals and there is strong coordination for the students, it is possible to organize such a program with considerable success. The following might be a sample guide for high school volunteers.

Guide for High School Volunteers

It is most important that you make a good impression in your initial meeting with the elementary school principal and the classroom teacher. The following suggestions are intended to help you feel comfortable in your role as "tutor":

- Be on time. Principals and teachers are busy people, and they are taking time out of their schedule in order to meet with you.
- Report to the main office every time you visit the school. Inform the secretary who you are and the time of your appointment.
- Dress neatly.
- Have your materials and your letter of assignment with you.
- Take some paper and a pencil with you in order to take notes.

- Be sure that at the end of the meeting you have the answers to the following questions:
    1. Where do I report when I come to the school?
    2. What time should I be at the school?
    3. Where is the room or area in which I will be teaching?
    4. Will a classroom teacher or aide be present?
    5. How will I "handle" problems that come up?
    6. How many students will be in the class?
    7. May I use the ditto machine? the overhead projector?
    8. Are there any school rules I should be aware of?
    9. What supplies or materials are available to me? How do I get the materials I need?
    10. Will the students have paper or a notebook and writing materials (depending on the grade level)?

In order for this type of program to have some degree of success, the peer "teachers" need training, they need a curriculum, they need access to a picture file, they need to be able to discuss problems with their high school teacher contact, they need to learn how to plan simple lessons, they need to know how to handle general classroom routines and difficulties, and they need to get recognition for their efforts and accomplishments. A certificate of some kind is appreciated.

If the emphasis is on a districtwide effort to promote foreign languages on all levels, this type of program helps both elementary school students and high school students. However, there must be agreement, by all persons concerned, that the FLEX program objectives are quite simple, and that in addition to the linguistic and cultural benefits, the elementary school youngsters are to be exposed to a pleasurable language learning experience. For an overview of this type of program, see Appendix C.

For additional information on the use of peer or cross-age tutors, see the Bibliography: Alcorn, 1; Barnett, 19; Koster, 92; and Lipton *et al.*, 109.

Adult volunteers (parents and members of the community) may be used in this type of program, but it must be remembered that there must be training sessions for these volunteers. Knowledge of and proficiency in the foreign language is not enough. Volunteers want and need training in classroom management, sequencing and pacing of lessons, lesson planning, planning effective and varied lessons, evaluating progress, reviewing and reinforcing concepts, etc. See the sample agenda on page 57 of a workshop for adult volunteers in a FLEX program.

TEACHER TRAINING

Preservice Training

During the preservice stage prospective FLES/FLEX/ immersion teachers would benefit from an orientation to the school system and to this age level. The ideal situation would be a university FLES/FLEX/immersion course given at the university or in the district, which would give the new teacher an introduction to the field and practice in the various components of lessons. A course currently offered at the University of Maryland/Baltimore County has the following session outline:

1. Rationale for FLES, FLEX, and immersion
2. Place of FLES, FLEX, and immersion in elementary school
3. Needs of elementary school youngsters: applications to teaching
4. Options in **FLES**: FLES, FLEX, immersion
5. Contrasting FLEX in elementary school and exploratory in middle school
6. Techniques for teaching listening comprehension skills
7. Techniques for teaching speaking skills
8. Techniques for teaching reading skills
9. Techniques for teaching writing skills
10. Overview of materials and their use; criteria for selection
11. Development of lesson plans: long-range, weekly, daily
12. Use of multimedia materials and equipment; relationship to the curriculum
13. Techniques for evaluating student progress and grading procedures, if required
14. Development of activities beyond the classroom

15. Techniques for teaching cultural components

Final examination

Other aspects of the course that should be noted are the presentation of short mini-lessons by the participants, evaluation of materials, review of the current research with an objective point of view, mock role-playing as members of boards of education or study committees, interviews with **FLES** and secondary school teachers, and many other activities. Guest speakers to the course representing different points of view and different bases of experience help participants to put all ideas in perspective.

The following represents the type of final examination that might be given at the completion of the FLES/FLEX/ immersion methods course; it demonstrates the skills and competencies essential for the successful teacher:

1. Assume that a Spanish-speaking parent comes to complain that her child is not learning anything new in Spanish sequential FLES. What do you say? What do you do?

2. Invent a significant question about FLES, FLEX and immersion and answer it. You will be graded on the quality of the question as well as the answer.

3. Describe three cultural concepts you would teach in FLES, FLEX, and immersion. Show how this would be different in each.

4. Write three lesson plans, with explanations, according to the following:

    1 lesson plan for grades 1–2 immersion
    1 lesson plan for grades 3–4 FLEX
    1 lesson plan for grades 5–6 sequential FLES

5. Discuss the contributions of five outstanding personalities mentioned during the course. Give specific ways in which FLES, FLEX, or immersion have been affected by these people because of what they have written, what they have proposed, etc.

6. What kinds of competencies should a teacher of FLES, FLEX, or immersion have? How are they different? What aspects of their training, personality, language skills, etc., should they have? Should there be any compromises?

7. Discuss the importance of listening comprehension in FLES, FLEX, and immersion. How does this skill relate to the other language skills? What is the current thought about listening comprehension? What activities can be planned to develop this skill?

While methodology is extremely important, use of the foreign language is paramount. Therefore, even in the methods course provision should be made for students to use the language laboratory, to join language clubs and tables designed for conversational practice, to listen to radio and television programs being broadcast in the target language, to read target language newspapers and magazines, in order to keep all the skills of foreign language communication sharply honed. The most dynamic, effective teacher cannot function well in the classroom unless his/her foreign language skills are maintained and continue to grow stronger. This applies to all foreign language teachers, whether they are teaching FLES, FLEX, or immersion.

Prospective teachers should be encouraged to join professional organizations so that they can attend conferences, receive professional journals and newsletters, and learn about current trends in the field.

Inservice Training

One successful way to provide inservice training for FLES/FLEX/immersion teachers is the institute approach. Institutes are held either during the summer or during the school year. A two- to three-week institute session held during the summer allows intensive practice in foreign language skills, and extensive cultural information can be imparted. If the foreign language is used around the clock in real-life day-to-day situations, participants will emerge from the experience with greater enthusiasm for the task and with a broad scope of additional knowledge. Harkening to the NDEA Institutes of the past, the current breed of teacher-training foreign language institutes are sensitive to the need for immersion in the foreign language as well as to the need for expansion of methodological skills.

The institute type of training is useful before service and for teachers already in service. Other types of inservice courses can be offered at the local level, devoted to the specific needs of the teachers. One such course may deal with the current analysis of the foreign culture(s); another may offer another introductory foreign language course (Spanish for teachers of French, for example); another may be the methods of teaching English for teachers of immersion; another may be a discussion of the new trends in listening and speaking skills. These courses may be taught by knowledgeable personnel within the school district or by university faculty. The major goal is to enrich, broaden, and enhance teachers' abilities and skills.

Periodic workshops with hands-on components are extremely helpful for teachers. Generally, it is a wise procedure to poll the teachers on their choice of workshop topics and presenters. Teachers respond more favorably to inservice programs when they have been involved in the planning. These one-day workshops help to inspire teachers during the school year and usually provide them with materials and activities to try out immediately with their classes.

Finally, a last word about teacher training. It is vital that teachers gain confidence about their own wisdom in making choices for their classes. The person who is "on the firing lines with students" is the teacher. Teachers need to learn about the theoretical bases for instruction, the pedagogical approaches and techniques, and the essentials of child psychology and growth. Teachers need to be open to new developments and practices in language learning, but they also need to rely on their own experience and the experience of colleagues in the field in order to implement effective practices in their own classrooms. Helping teachers see a wide range of options and bolster their own self-confidence in making decisions are the ultimate goals of teacher training programs.

SCHEDULING

In order to implement the program selected, decisions have to be made about the number of sessions per week and number of minutes per session. Other questions need answers, such as: will the class have an itinerant teacher or a regular classroom teacher? How many classes will each teacher teach? Will there be planning time for the **FLES** teacher and the classroom teacher(s)? One caution, however. In the sixties, teachers who were itinerant often taught more than 150 students each day, neither getting to know the students nor being able to deliver satisfactory programs with such a heavy load. Teaching schedules must be cost-effective, but they must take into account the very real and pressing problems this schedule might cause.

Very frequently, the crucial problem in scheduling is the question (for sequential FLES and FLEX) of which aspects of the elementary school curriculum will be left out. There are few simple answers to this question, but often, if teachers and administrators earnestly try to find time in an extremely crowded schedule, it is possible to find 30 to 60 minutes a week. More efficiency in class movements, more correlation with subjects already being taught such as social studies and language arts, more flexibility from the sort of rigid schedule shown on page 58, more functional use of opening and closing routines, and so on, would open up the schedule a little. The difficulty is getting a consensus of all parties. In this respect, immersion programs have the advantage, since the foreign language is incorporated into the teaching of the basic subjects in the elementary school curriculum.

A RECIPE FOR THE FLES* TEACHER WHO WANTS TO GET RAVE REVIEWS!

I was asked, some time ago, to provide a "recipe" for a **FLES** teacher that might ensure success—something that would get **FLES** teachers "rave reviews," based on my experience and observations. The following is the recipe, but as every good cook knows, a recipe can and should be adapted to individual tastes (or, in this case, to the individual **FLES** teacher's taste and sense of teaching style):

Blend the following ingredients:
    4 cups Planning
    5 cups Teaching Performance (exciting, effective, enthusiastic, enjoyable, and empathetic to the children)

4 cups Pace, Tempo, Variety, Flexibility in Teaching
5 cups Personality and Rapport with Students
2 cups Humor
2 cups Joie de Vivre and Charm
Sprinkle generously with Understanding and Patience
Pack all of the above ingredients (all 22 cups) into an attractive container, decorated with all the trimmings.

What will you get? You'll get "rave reviews"!!

WHERE TO FIND ASSISTANCE

A word about where to look for assistance. The study committee may seek advice from secondary school teachers of foreign languages, from knowledgeable members of the community, from language teachers at local colleges and universities, and from the following agencies:

Information	A.C.T.F.L. (American Council on the Teaching of Foreign Languages) 579 Broadway Hastings-on-Hudson, NY 10706
Information	American Association of Teachers of French 57 Armory Ave. Champaign, IL 61820
Information	M.L.A. (Modern Language Association) 10 Astor Place New York, NY 10003
Assistance and Information	National FLES/FLEX/Immersion Commission of A.A.T.F. University of Maryland/Baltimore County Dept. Modern Languages/Linguistics (M.L.L.) Catonsville, MD 21228
Newsletter and Information Research	National Network for Early Language Learning and C.A.L. (Center for Applied Linguistics) 1118 22 St., NW Washington, DC 20037

Information for Parents	A.L.L. (Advocates for Language Learning) Box 4964 Culver City, CA 90231
Information and Research	C.L.E.A.R. (Center for Language Education and Research) 1100 Glendon Ave. Los Angeles, CA 90024
Research and Publications	Ontario Institute for Studies in Education 252 Bloor St. W. Toronto, Ontario M5S IVs, Canada

---

HIGHLIGHTS

- **Set your goals *first***
- **Develop a program that matches your goals**
- **If it does not work, go back and readjust various aspects of the program**
- **Be realistic!**

CONTRACT
FOR STUDENT INSTRUCTORS IN THE FLEX PROGRAM

AS A STUDENT INSTRUCTOR IN THE FLEX PROGRAM SPONSORED BY THE FOREIGN LANGUAGE DEPARTMENT OF _____ HIGH SCHOOL, I AGREE TO ABIDE BY THE FOLLOWING PRINCIPLES:

a) TO BECOME FAMILIAR ENOUGH WITH THE SCHOOL IN WHICH I AM PLACED SO AS TO OBSERVE *ALL* SCHOOL RULES AND REGULATIONS

b) TO WORK CLOSELY WITH MY COOPERATING TEACHER AND TO OBSERVE *ALL* CLASSROOM RULES SET BY HIM/HER

c) TO BE RESPONSIBLE ENOUGH TO MAINTAIN AN EXCELLENT ATTENDANCE AND PUNCTUALITY RECORD

d) TO DEVELOP A GOOD WORKING RELATIONSHIP WITH MY COOPERATING TEACHER AND WITH MY STUDENTS

e) TO MAINTAIN A POSITIVE ATTITUDE TOWARD MY STUDENTS, MY COOPERATING TEACHER, THE SCHOOL PRINCIPAL, AND OTHER STAFF MEMBERS AT THE SCHOOL

f) TO DEMONSTRATE MY EXTENSIVE KNOWLEDGE OF MATERIAL THROUGH *CAREFUL* AND *THOROUGH* PLANNING OF ACTIVITIES FOR MY STUDENTS

g) TO EXECUTE MY PLANS IN A WELL-ORGANIZED AND AN EFFECTIVE MANNER

_____
Student Volunteer

_____
Chair, High School
Foreign Language Department

_____
Principal, Elementary School

Sample Workshop for Adult Volunteers in the FLEX Program

AGENDA

1. Greetings and introductions
2. Overview of the FLEX program
3. Schedules and time allotments
4. Materials of instruction: demonstration of books, syllabus, tapes, pictures, charts, etc.
5. Break
6. Demonstration: Teaching a shock language (this may be Russian, Korean, Vietnamese, etc.)
7. Post-Demonstration Discussion
   How did you feel?
   What did you learn?
   Did you need more repetitions?
   Did the pictures help? Did the gestures help?
   Do you understand what you were saying?
8. Tips for teaching new work
9. Tips for teaching a song, a dialogue, a poem
10. Concerns, questions, comments
11. Topics requested for next workshop

A Sample Daily Elementary School Schedule

Is there room for foreign language?
(These schedules may vary from school district to school district.)

		M	T	W	TH	F
9:00	Opening Routines					
9:10–11:25	Language Arts Reading Spelling Writing/Composition Handwriting Literature	Art 10:00–11:00	Music 11:45–12:15	P.E. 10:30–11:00		
11:30–12:15	Mathematics					
12:15–1:15	Lunch and Activities					
1:15–2:00	Social Studies					P.E. 1:15–2:45
2:05–2:50	Science				Music 2:05–2:35	
2:50–3:00	Closing Routines					

GUIDELINES:

Math	195 minutes
Science	195 minutes
Social Studies	195 minutes

Language Arts	600 minutes
Reading	300 minutes
Writing/Comp.	120 minutes
Spelling	80 minutes
Handwriting	40 minutes
Literature	60 minutes

Art	60 minutes
Music	60 minutes
P.E.	60 minutes

V

What Is the Content of FLES*?

The content of FLES and FLEX covers a wide range, depending on the goals of the program. In immersion, the content *is* the elementary school curriculum, taught through the foreign language.

In FLES and FLEX, dialogues, narratives and stories, questions and answers, riddles, jokes, poems, songs, and conversational patterns of all kinds can be the basis for the linguistic and cultural content. But teachers (and students) soon find out that following only one approach soon leads to boredom on the part of the children (and probably the teacher, too!). The following will be a discussion of some of the basic approaches in FLES and FLEX in organizing the content or curriculum: the dialogue approach, the story or narrative approach, the question/answer–command/action approach, the situation or thematic approach, and the content-enriched and content-based approaches.

THE DIALOGUE APPROACH

Using a dialogue approach, basic structures, vocabulary, and idiomatic expressions can be used and practiced in the context of a specific topic or conversation. It can be a conversation between two or more people in a natural setting, reflecting the interests of the students. Hopefully, it will contain some significant cultural aspects or implications, including gestures and customs. An effective dialogue is one that can be adapted to new and different settings while using the basic structures.

Teaching the Dialogue

- Brief presentation in the foreign language and/or English indicating the setting, the characters, and perhaps some motivational questions asking students to listen for some action or outcome.

- Presentation of the dialogue, with the teacher reciting the lines, and pointing to puppets, children, pictures representing each character. Use of gestures, and actions is essential if students are to get the gist of the dialogue and some meaning and comprehension.

- The next step is for the teacher to present some of the new vocabulary through pictures, actions, gestures, and props. (Explanation in English when necessary.)

- A second presentation, having children act out the action, or using a filmstrip, magnetboard, or flannelboard provides more familiarity with the dialogue.

- Class repetition of the lines of the dialogue would follow next, with subsequent half-class repetitions, small-group repetitions, and partner repetitions. There is considerable controversy over whether every dialogue must be memorized. Memorization of some dialogues certainly does give youngsters a repertoire of conversational settings, but particularly at the fifth and sixth grade levels, children show a reluctance to memorize everything. The effective teacher will probably prefer to have only some of the dialogues memorized, while the others can be read aloud.

- Depending on the age and grade level and experience with the foreign language, the next step (or simultaneous with the previous step) will be for the students to see a written copy of the dialogue. Careful attention should be directed by the teacher to the sound-letter correspondences and discrepancies (e.g., which are the silent letters, written but not pronounced?).

- Next, teachers (with assistance and suggestions from students) would alter the dialogue by changing the subjects, by adding new vocabulary, and by changing the idiomatic expressions.

Suggestions for the Adaptation of Dialogues

Teachers often find out, by direct and indirect means, what the youngsters are talking about in the course of their daily experience. Teachers should find out which topics are being covered in social studies, science, family living, and health education (to name a few) during the rest of the school day. Teacher should find out which stories, books, and magazines the children are reading, both in and out of school. Teachers should discover which songs they like to sing and listen to (rock and roll, country, etc.) as well as which television programs they like to watch.

The main purpose for all this detective work is for teachers to understand the children better and to try to develop a language program that reflects the preferred "environment" of the students. The names of singers, actors and actresses, songs, etc., will affect the content of the FLES and FLEX program. How much better to use the names of famous singers in a dialogue, than to use María and José. How much more interesting to include space travel in a conversation than to use an ordinary travel pattern. This is not to say that typical day-to-day dialogues should not be an important part of the curriculum! I merely wish to point out that repetition, which is indispensable in FLES and FLEX, has to have periodic relief by way of interesting topics, humor, and surprise as well as reality and fantasy.

For example, after a standard dialogue about travel has been presented and learned, why not branch out?

EVITA: So, you're leaving for the moon?
JORGE: Sure. My rocket ship is ready.
EVITA: Isn't it dangerous to go to the moon?
JORGE: Not very.
EVITA: Well then, I'm going too!

In future repetitions, instead of going to the moon, students could opt for going to Jupiter, Mars, Venus—or Spain, Mexico, or Panama. Instead of dangerous, it could be amusing, boring, exciting, "cool." Instead of "I'm going too," it could be "I'm going to read a book," or "I'm going to watch a video," or whatever.

Some drills are necessary, although not quite so extensive as in the **FLES** programs of the 1960s. Effective techniques should not be abandoned just because they were popular twenty years ago. With discretion, they can still be used. Here are a few drills:

Repetition drills: Children repeat the content, following the teacher model or a student model.

Substitution drills: Children substitute different components. For example:

> Your are going to *the moon?*
> You are going to *Paris?*
> You are going to *Mars?*

Or: *Neil Armstrong is* going to the moon.

Or: Neil Armstrong *went* to the moon.

Or: My rocket ship is ready.
> *My sister* is ready.
> *My brother* is ready.
> *My father* is ready.

Transformation drills:

> I *am going* to the moon.
> I *went* to the moon.
>
> My brother is ready.
> My brother is *not* ready.
> *Is* your brother ready?

After the dialogue is learned, teachers may wish to ask comprehension questions and/or ask personalized questions of the students (e.g., Do you like apples?) based on the likes and dislikes expressed in the dialogue. It is imperative that youngsters get a chance to use questions, too, either asking questions of other students or of the teacher.

Children like to role-play or dramatize the dialogue when they feel comfortable with it. They particularly enjoy moving out of the original dialogue and shaping it according to their own imagination. This step is vital, so that students can learn how to say in the foreign language their own ideas, humor, expressions— within the limits of what they can absorb. They may want to go far afield, and the teacher has to narrow the range and simplify their expressions at early levels. They have more opportunities to express themselves in the immersion sequence because they have spent enormous blocks of time using the foreign language as a tool of learning. However, even in FLES/FLEX, with less time devoted to the foreign language, it is essential that children begin to feel the power of expressing their own thoughts in the foreign language. (See the section "Dramatizing and Role-Playing" in Chapter 7.)

The Dialogue Approach in Immersion

While the dialogue approach is generally not used in immersion to teach the language, it is often used to practice the language and concepts in social studies, for example. A dialogue developed by the children to illustrate the discoveries of Cortez in Mexico would enhance the important concepts.

The dialogue approach can also be applied to the development of higher-order thinking skills. For example, if the dialogue deals with taking a trip, students could be asked to categorize which articles they would take to travel to Argentina in July, for example. They could then be asked to contrast the type of clothing they would pack to travel to Spain in July.

A final word about the dialogue approach is essential at this point. Because many teachers in the past insisted that their students memorize every dialogue, memorizing is currently subject to some loss of acceptance. Here again I must stress that it is *not* necessary to discard effective practices because they may no longer be in the current educational vogue. Based on my experience and on the observation of hundreds of successful teachers, I am convinced that dialogues have value, and should be included in the broad range of approaches used by the **FLES** teacher.

THE STORY OR NARRATIVE APPROACH (FOR FLEX, FLES, AND IMMERSION)

The advantage of using a story approach is that it enables the teacher to use or adapt authentic folk tales that reflect the foreign culture. The steps for presenting the story are similar to those for the dialogue: clarification and presentation; presentation of new words and expressions; repetition and memorization (rarely); comprehension check; questions on the story; questions personalized to the children; adaptation of the story with introduction of additional vocabulary, verbs, adjectives, adverbs, etc.

Additional steps with the story approach would be the development of the cultural content through additional pictures; map and globe studies to identify the locale; discussion of the effects of geography and weather on the life of the people in the story; cross-cultural contrasting between the family life in the foreign culture in the story and that in the United States; role-playing not only parts of the story but also life in the foreign culture as depicted or inferred by the children; checking on false assumptions by questions and research or defending assumptions based upon some parts of the story, etc. Naturally, the more sophisticated activities will be limited to immersion students in grades 4, 5, and 6 or upper-level (grades 5 and 6) FLES students.

The most important reason for using the narrative or story approach for FLES, FLEX, and immersion is that through this approach, the listening skills are developed and enhanced. It gives the teacher many opportunities to read to the students and play recordings of stories so that the children hear different voices using the foreign language. It is not always necessary to complete the story in one class lesson. I used to read a story, and when I came to the most exciting part, I would stop and indicate that we would finish the story on the following day. This technique (used by radio and television producers!) works wonders for student motivation.

An excellent example of the story or narrative approach can be found in Chase, 33.

THE QUESTION/ANSWER–COMMAND/ACTION APPROACH (FOR FLES AND FLEX)

This approach has as its advantage the fact that the curriculum contains the evaluation items. Just like any other approach or curriculum, if it is used as the sole procedure, boredom will rapidly set in. From time to time, particularly at early stages of FLES/FLEX, some of the following topics and activities will be included:

classroom objects	greetings
colors	telling time

numbers   weather
family   days of the week
clothing   months and seasons

Other times, when a FLEX program is introduced, a question/ answer–command/action approach can limit the scope of the curriculum (while still affording expansion if the ability of the students warrants it). Following are excerpts from a 30-week course of study based on this approach. It was first used in order to control the content in an experimental study I conducted, but it has been modified for use elsewhere.

While there were only fifteen questions listed for each six-week period, teachers were urged to slot in different nouns and verbs where possible. The questions from one unit were periodically reviewed (and the responses retaught, if necessary). Youngsters asked each other questions and asked the teachers questions. They also gave some of the commands.

Although it is possible to inject some humor and imagination into a curriculum of this kind, it is a far cry from a real-life, natural curriculum, unless there is time to make adaptations in depth.

The responses expected to these questions will vary: sometimes a complete sentence; sometimes several words; sometimes one-word answers other than "yes" or "no." After learning basic responses, children can be encouraged to respond in different, personalized ways.

Sample FLEX Unit (1)

(approx. 6 weeks)

Topics covered: Greetings, Introductions, Days of the Week, Health, Attendance, Weather, Numbers 1–10, Addition, Subtraction

1. Où est le professeur?
2. Comment vous appelez-vous?

3. Où sont les élèves?

4. Qui est absent?

5. Quel jour de la semaine est-ce aujourd'hui?

6. Ça va bien?

7. Comment allez-vous?

8. Qui est malade?

9. Combien font deux et trois?

10. Combien font six moins deux?

11. Combien d'élèves y a-t-il dans la classe?

12. Comment s'appelle-t-il?

13. Comment s'appelle-t-elle?

14. Allez au professeur.*

15. Quel temps fait-il aujourd'hui?

Sample FLEX Unit (2)

(approx. 6 weeks)

Topics covered: Classroom Objects, Colors, Time, Commands

1. Allex à la porte.*

2. Levez-vous.*

3. Où est le livre?

4. Où sont les fenêtres?

5. De quelle couleur est le papier?

6. Comptez les crayons.

7. Asseyez-vous.*

8. Quel temps fait-il?

9. Qu'est-ce que c'est?

*Action or total physical response

10. Quelle heure est-il?

11. Combien font dix fois deux?

12. Touchez la craie.*

13. Est-ce l'horloge?

14. Le cahier est rouge?

15. Il est deux heures et demie?

Sample FLEX Unit (3)

(approx. 6 weeks)

Topics covered: Review Commands; Additional Commands, Possessives with Classroom Objects, Members of the Family, Age, *est-ce que*

1. Mettez le livre dans le pupitre.*

2. Comment est votre grand-mère?

3. Quel âge avez-vous?

4. Dessinez votre soeur.*

5. Prenez le stylo.*

6. Asseyez-vous.*

7. Donnez-moi la carte.*

8. Allez à votre place.*

9. Combien de personnes y a-t-il dans votre famille?

10. Combien d'élèves dans la classe?

11. Levez-vous.*

12. Quel âge a ton chien?

13. Est-ce que le père est un homme?

14. Est-ce son livre?

15. Qui est beau?

*Action or total physical response

THE SITUATION OR THEMATIC APPROACH (FOR FLES AND FLEX)

Depending on the initial grade of instruction, a FLES or FLEX thematic approach or curriculum will move through three or more years of sequential, spiral learning, with each year reviewing and expanding previous work as well as introducing additional themes. For example, a three-year curriculum might include some of the following topics:

Year One

School Greetings, days of the week, name-equivalents in the foreign languages, classroom objects, colors, numbers, weather, time

Family Members, age, pets, names, relationships

Occupations Names, places of business

House Different types of homes, rooms, furniture

Year Two

Clothing Articles of clothing, colors, plurals

Toys Different types of toys, colors, activities, games

Home Expansion of rooms, furniture, activities in the home, pets and other animals

Food Different types of food, meals, plurals, likes and dislikes, telling time, numbers

Neighborhood Buildings, different places, directions

Year Three

Going to a restaurant Expansion of food, ordering meals, amenities in a restaurant

Going shopping	Shopping for food, shopping for clothing, shopping for toys
Travel	Visiting relatives, taking longer trips; expansion of occupations connected with travel
Entertainment and recreation	Movies, sports, seasonal activities

Included in this thematic curriculum must be the necessary vocabulary, idiomatic expressions, verbs, adjectives, adverbs, and exclamations with which to build dialogues, stories, questions and answers, personalized items suggested by the children and other local interests and activities. If the local community boasts a football team, then many of the language activities will focus on the team and its goings and comings. If the community sponsors an exchange program, then there will be many opportunities for developing cross-cultural contrasts, particularly with day-to-day activities.

However, no matter which themes are included in the FLES/FLEX curriculum, the most important goal is to give children the opportunity to use what they have learned—first in familiar situations, but then in unfamiliar situations. For example, after a unit on going shopping has been completed, students might be given the following situation:

Setting: You are shopping for food for dinner with your friend. You have the equivalent of $8.00. The total for what you want to buy is the equivalent of $10.50.

Task: What would you say to your friend? What would you say to the vendor? What would you do?

In order to deal effectively with the problem, students need to be able to use numbers, names of food items, courtesy expressions, etc., in a real-life situation. Many other situations could be developed by the teacher and the students, too, which could be placed in a box. Periodically, youngsters would select one of the situations for performance. At first, the children might rehearse the situation; later on, groups of children might be able to perform on an impromptu basis. This procedure can also be very effective in evaluating student proficiency and/or in diagnosing the need for review, reteaching, or further drill and practice.

Many teachers may ask about standards of accuracy in usage and pronunciation skills. That depends on the time of year, on the specific purpose of the proficiency activity, on what the instructions are, on the audience (if any), etc. If it is a more practiced activity, then the teacher will want to take careful notes (and ask the students in the audience to do so, as well) in order to suggest corrections, since obviously there are no correct or incorrect answers for a given situation. On the other hand, if this is the first attempt on the part of the children, as long as everyone understands what is being said (that is, as long as communication is taking place) the teacher may not want to stifle expression.

Here are additional suggestions for situations:

- Your dog has run away.
- You are eating at a friend's house and they serve something you detest.
- Your friend has just broken your new toy.
- You are at the dentist's office with a terrible toothache, but you are frightened.
- You fall off your chair in a restaurant.
- You are introducing your friend to your mother and you forget your friend's name.
- You spill your container of popcorn in the movies.
- You get lost at the airport.
- You get on the bus and you do not have the correct change.
- You did not do your homework.
- You are at the zoo and you get sick.

THE CONTENT-ENRICHED AND THE CONTENT-BASED APPROACHES (FOR FLES, FLEX, AND IMMERSION)

The goals for the development of skills and abilities in the elementary school curriculum can be achieved through the other subjects studied *and* **FLES**. Such skills and abilities as oral and written communication and self-expression, the learning of language concepts, reading and writing skills, and understanding the meaning of symbols and abstract ideas (to name a few) can all be integrated to some degree, with the study of the basic vocabulary and expressions of the target language in a content-enriched approach.

In the area of language arts, children in **FLES** can be encouraged to

- read books about the the foreign culture in English
- see the roots of the foreign language in English in such words as *chauffeur, fiesta,* and *kindergarten*
- write and prepare assembly programs on themes about the target culture
- read about the lives of famous people from the target culture
- write letters to pen pals in the foreign culture
- dramatize international events and folk tales
- research various aspects of the foreign culture by reading, interviewing, writing for information, etc.
- set up displays about the foreign culture
- go on field trips (to museums, restaurants, etc.)
- discuss current events in the foreign culture
- listen to and speak with guest speakers from the foreign culture
- write letters of appreciation to guest speakers

In the area of social studies, children in **FLES** can be encouraged to

- enhance their map skills by identifying the location of areas where the foreign language is spoken
- discover place names in the United States that have foreign origins, such as Montpelier and Laredo
- study a unit on early explorers from the foreign culture
- research the contributions of people in the foreign culture to the American Revolution, the United Nations, etc.

- explore these topics in the foreign culture for similarities to and differences from our own:
  - family life
  - politics
  - kinesics
  - media
  - role of men and women
  - attitudes toward money, land, humor, food, etc.
  - careers and occupations
  - leisure activities, such as sports, TV, etc.
  - geography and history
  - institutions
  - architecture
  - religion
  - food, nutrition, cuisine
  - ceremonies, customs, and rituals
  - taboos and superstitions
  - science, mathematics and technology
  - other topics

- learn similarities and differences in concepts and vocabulary. For example, the word *bread* may have different conceptual bases from *le pain* in French, *el pan* in Spanish, etc.

- identify the contributions of the foreign culture to English through borrowed words and expressions

- compare holiday celebrations in the United States and in the foreign culture

- discuss current political events in the foreign culture

- identify gestures and meaning in the United States and the foreign culture

- discuss person-to-person relationships in the family and outside the family (including the use of the familiar forms in the foreign language) and personal distance for comfortable conversations in different cultures, etc.

- explore the origin of customs and ceremonies in the target culture and the significance of the symbols and colors on the flags of different countries

Similarly, other subjects in the elementary school curriculum can be enriched:

- Art projects similar to projects in the foreign culture can be worked on, such as weaving, etc.
- Music offers all kinds of folk songs, popular music, etc.
- Physical education offers games, sports, folk dances, etc.
- Mathematics and science include the study and origin of the metric system, the rate of exchange of foreign currency, famous mathematicians and scientists, etc.

For more information on the interdisciplinary aspects of **FLES**, see Chapter 6. See the Bibliography: Bragaw *et al.*, 26; Damen, 37; Donoghue, 47; Elementary, 55; Flaitz, 61; Green, 75; Griffin, 76; Joiner, 89; Seelye, 182; Sparkman, 190; Stern, 193; and Wallace and Wirth, 214.

The Content-Based Approach

This is one of the newer approaches to **FLES**, based upon the success of various immersion programs. With the content-based approach, a unit of social studies, for example, is taught entirely or partially in the foreign language, making certain that all the necessary vocabulary and expressions are understood by the children. Through this approach, the youngsters learn new concepts in subject matter, as well as foreign language components in all four skills.

Sample Content-Based Unit, Grade 4

(approximately 3 weeks)

1. Directions: north, south, east, west.
   Crossing rivers, oceans, lakes, mountains, plains
2. Travel by means of train, car, bus, plane, bicycle, and on foot

Looking at a map of the United States, Canada, and Mexico, students and teacher could make various statements about directions (all in the foreign language):

Here is the United States on the map.

Here is Canada, to the north of the United States.

Here is Mexico, to the south of the United States.

Washington is the capital of the United States.

Mexico City is the capital of Mexico.

The president of the United States is _____.

The president of Mexico is _____.

Students then could dictate an experience story about a boy and a girl traveling from San Francisco to Mexico City, crossing rivers, lakes, mountains, plains.

Students, in groups, could then describe the trip, using different types of transportation: train, car, bus, plane, bicycle, and on foot. They could make scrapbooks for the group, showing a map, places visited en route, road signs they would pass, etc., depending on the information they received while doing research in several Spanish books in class.

As a culmination, each group could dramatize one aspect of the trip (amusing or historical in nature, or demonstrating some of the difficulties encountered, etc.). This would help reinforce the social studies concepts as well as the functional use of Spanish.

The content selected for foreign language in the elementary school depends on the goals of the program. But it also depends on the abilities of the youngsters, the resources and materials, the teachers, the schedule, and what is a realistic expectation leading to some degree of proficiency.

The content of FLES/FLEX is by no means limited to those forms of organization of content described above. Some others come to mind:

- Holidays in the foreign culture
- Video, film, computer programs
- A mini-trip to the foreign culture
- A joint foreign language/social studies unit (e.g. a unit in French/a unit on Canada or a unit in Spanish/a unit on Latin America)

- Total physical response
- A combination of all those already mentioned
- Letters and tapes sent to and received from pen pals in the foreign culture
- Foods in different cultures
- Songs in the foreign culture

The curriculum is the organization of the content. It must be vitalized by an enthusiastic teacher using a broad range of teaching techniques appropriate to the age and abilities of the youngsters in his/her class. Essentially, however, if a FLES/FLEX program is to be successful, there must be a long-range curriculum in which the specific content is spelled out in detail.

CONTENT AT THE KINDERGARTEN–GRADE 3 LEVEL

Content at this early level moves slowly, devotes shorter periods of time to the foreign language in FLES and FLEX, and has very short segments of the lesson. Since children's attention span is brief at this level, teachers find that they must change activities every 3 to 4 minutes in a 20-minute lesson. Activities alternately change from listening and being seated to moving around or singing and dancing or role-playing. The content revolves around the children's daily activities at school and at home, including pets and animals in the zoo. They like number and counting games, and reading readiness activities. By grade three, they can apply some of the word-attack skills they have learned in English to reading in the foreign language, but they need special instructions when it comes to sound-letter correspondences. The content of a lesson in Grade 1 might include

- Numbers 1–11; counting with a ball
- Telling time
- Using toy clock to tell time
- Movement to illustrate the arms of the clock at various times of the day

- Listening to a story
- Playing "live" tic-tac-toe (children standing on X or O places in the classroom)

CONTENT AT GRADES 4–6

The content at grades 4 to 6, depending on when the foreign language was started, would be on a more sophisticated level and would follow the topics listed earlier. There would be reading and writing activities, and some of the movement activities would be successful at this level, too, such as "live" tic-tac-toe. The content of a lesson in grade 5, for example, in a class which had started in grade 4, might include:

- Reviewing numbers 1–31
- Learning to tell time
- Playing "Buzz"
- Working on a worksheet on time, writing in the time as pictured
- Listening to a story
- Dramatizing the story
- Reading parts of the story
- Writing answers to questions about the story
- Discussing time for meals in the U.S. and in the foreign culture

CONTENT IN IMMERSION PROGRAMS

The foreign language content in immersion programs revolves around the daily use of the foreign language for the purpose of communication and instruction. Even at early grades, teachers focus on the sound system, on phonics, and on reading readiness activities. In grades 2 and 3, word-attack skills in the foreign language are developed and practiced, as well as reading and writing activities appropriate for the regular elementary school curriculum. Specific terms and vocabulary in the foreign language are presented to facilitate instruction in the content areas of social studies, science and math, and other areas. Because science and math are manipulative, the children get more time for these subjects in grades 1, 2, and 3. Basically, the content in immersion programs is controlled by the district elementary school curriculum, and so much of this content is supposed to mirror what other children in the same grade level are studying in English, except that immersion students complete grade 6 also being functionally fluent in the foreign language.

Immersion programs also provide a focus on English language skills, depending on when they are introduced. Many of the programs introduce English in grade 3, while the content of the elementary school program is continued through the medium of the foreign language. When immersion programs delay the introduction of English language arts until grade 4 or even grade 5, parents worry about students' progress in reading and spelling. Research studies indicate that some students will experience some lag in English language skills—language arts and reading (Dulay *et al.*, 50; Genesee, 68)—but that most of them will make up these deficiencies in English by the end of the elementary school grades. Concerning differences in achievement in second-language reading, Genesee (68, 69) indicated that these differences may be due to "grade level, student ability, socioeconomic status and other factors." In view of my own experience with bilingual and immersion programs, I recommend that English skills be started *no later than* grade 3 in immersion programs.

HIGHLIGHTS

- **The content is dependent upon the goals of the program**

- **The selection of the type of organization of the content is also based on the goals**

- **Following only *one* approach to the exclusion of others may lead to boredom**

VI

Teaching the Four Skills
and Culture

INTRODUCTION TO THE DEVELOPMENT
OF THE SKILLS

Historically, there has been an interrelationship among the four skills of listening, speaking, reading, and writing. It was always rather difficult to teach each of the skills in isolation. That is why various approaches and methodologies combined two or more of the skills. For example, in the grammar-translation method, reading and writing were emphasized. During the audiolingual phase, listening and speaking were stressed, although reading and writing were included. The current vogue is to stress listening comprehension first before developing speaking, reading, and writing, which is an adaptation of the eclectic approach devoted to the four skills and culture.

With the research work of Krashen and Terrell (95), and Dulay *et al.* (50), and others, there is a new emphasis on active listening comprehension, but not to the exclusion of the other skills. The emphasis takes the form of delaying some of the other skills. It is a bit dismaying, however, for **FLES** teachers (myself included) to be told that it is essential to have a "silent period" of 50 hours or several months before their students should be asked to speak the foreign language. It has been my experience and that of many other experienced teachers of foreign language on the elementary school level that children love to imitate and thoroughly enjoy speaking the foreign language as early as possible in their instructional program. Many **FLES** teachers report consistently that their students, after only a week or two, are eager to play the role of the teacher in a variety of activities, games, TPR instructions, etc. This is not to say that the results of careful research under controlled conditions should be ignored. This is to say that the successful experience of many, many educators who are experienced teachers of foreign languages on the elementary school level should not be ignored!

For those interested in the current research on listening comprehension, consult Gass and Madden, 67; Krashen, 94; Krashen and Terrell, 95; Met, 143; Swain, 203; Ur, 207; and Wing, 220. Time will tell whether this method provides the correct direction. One of my concerns with urging teachers to delay other skills is that it brings to mind another time, the audiolingual era, when only listening and speaking were encouraged for at least 100 clock hours, and teachers were ordered not to have their students read or write in the foreign language.

The best approach for teachers is to be informed of the current research and theory, and to make decisions based on their experience, their own observations of student abilities and needs, and the goals of the foreign language program.

What follows will be brief guidelines for the development of the four skills and culture.

LISTENING COMPREHENSION SKILLS

Once thought to be a skill subservient to the speaking skill, in recent years the listening skill has been acclaimed as an important, significant skill in itself. Some research studies have proclaimed that the listening skill must precede the speaking skill for a specific period of time in order to saturate the brain with "comprehensible input." This will be contrasted with standard FLES/FLEX methodology in the next section.

During the heyday of audiolingualism, listening and speaking skills were twinned, although the theory and practice dictated that first the child listened and understood; next the child was asked to produce speech; reading and writing skills were postponed for at least 100 clock hours. In many **FLES** programs this meant at least one year solely of listening and speaking activities. A study was conducted in 1969, using the same grade 4 content but different methodology. The control group followed the "no reading, no writing" approach for one year; the experimental group was introduced to reading and writing after one day of listening and speaking presentations and practice. At the end of one year, both groups were tested on their listening comprehension skills. The results indicated that there was significant superiority of the experimental group. While not conclusive, the results certainly suggested that there was an interrelationship among the four skills. This study, conducted by me (119) was contrary to the then highly touted audiolingual delay in the introduction of reading and writing skills, particularly in **FLES**.

From that era evolved an eclectic approach (in this case, the four skills approach) giving almost equal importance to each skill. Practitioners have always thought the listening skill to be of great importance, particularly with "incidental learning," as it was called. Teachers used the foreign language extensively and found that some students "picked up" often-repeated words, phrases, idiomatic expressions, and intonation.

Within the last five years, the skills of active listening have come into their own. Termed the "forgotten skill," research and theories have placed it on a pedestal of prime importance. Currently, teachers are urged to promote listening comprehension ("comprehensible input") and to postpone their students' speaking performance for an undetermined period of time. The pendulum will probably swing back to some middle-ground position, giving once again almost equal importance to each of the four skills, and leaving decisions to the practitioner. Some of the factors that will determine which skills to stress might include the following:

- Goals of the program
- Curriculum objectives
- Abilities of the class
- Text and other materials in FLES/FLEX/immersion

- Place of the program in the foreign language sequence
- Expectations of FL teachers on the next level
- Text and other materials on the secondary school level
- Expectations of supervisors and parents
- Teacher preferences based on recent training and inservice
- Other local factors

The "how" of teaching foreign languages will vary from teacher to teacher, from school district to school district, etc. The bottom line is probably not which method nor which approach is used. The bottom line *is* the effectiveness of the teacher in motivating youngsters to learn and enjoy the learning process, as well as its results. The bottom line is concerned with results. What are the students able to do in the foreign language?

CONTRASTING STANDARD FLES/FLEX METHODOLOGY AND "COMPREHENSIBLE INPUT" METHODOLOGY

Standard or traditional FLES/FLEX methodology has its roots in the audiolingual approach to teaching foreign languages. Primarily, the emphasis is on listening and speaking skills right from the start, although all four skills are developed in varying degrees. There is stress on repetition, drills of all kinds, manipulation of language—thus emphasis on input and output. The content is limited, but dialogue situations abound, particularly those of interest to young children.

With the "Comprehensible Input" approach, developed by Krashen and Terrell (95), the most important element at the beginning is listening to get meaning or comprehension. Students are not asked to repeat or drill or manipulate the language. They are encouraged to listen, understand, and demonstrate through actions that they have understood. Some research has shown that when speaking is delayed, the understanding mode builds up a background of language, and later, speech emerges without formal instruction. Here, the emphasis is on input at the beginning, and later, on input and output. It puts less pressure on the students at the beginning, by delaying the time for them to produce language utterances. The content is limited, and real-life situations are extremely important in this approach.

Both of these approaches are useful in FLES/FLEX models. I strongly believe that it would be foolish to throw out approaches that have been successful in the past, although some modifications, to be sure, are necessary. Whether one calls it an eclectic approach, or a "best of all worlds" model, it is important to hold fast to methods that show results, and to vary *all* methods to keep motivation and interest high.

Here are some listening comprehension activities that may be conducted by the teacher.

- Words and phrases tied to actions
- Words and phrases tied to visual "props"
- Telling a story with pictures or the flannelboard
- Performing a skit with puppets
- Giving TPR commands (e.g., stand, go to Steve, shake hands, etc.)
- Playing an action game (e.g., Simple Simon)
- Answering questions with actions (e.g., what was Sleeping Beauty doing?)
- Reading a familiar folk tale by the Grimm brothers, with youngsters pantomiming the story

Children can be encouraged to participate in the following activities:

- Discriminating between similar and dissimilar sounds
- Interacting physically with commands, new vocabulary, etc.
- Listening to a taped story (perhaps recorded by classmates)
- Listening to songs in the FL (record, cassette, etc.)
- Listening to a skit on videotape
- Listening to a dialogue on film
- Taking a test on listening comprehension
- Following instructions (folding papers, placing books, etc.)

- Writing a spot dictation or full dictation
- Listening to a wide range of voices in the FL, in person and on tape
- Listening to radio forecasts on the weather; sports announcements; etc.
- Listening to different sounds on tape (familiar and unfamiliar)

A wide variety of activities can be devised that combine listening comprehension and motion or one or more of the other language skills. The teacher, however, will want to be alert to youngsters' listening comprehension skills, and if necessary, will plan activities that foster more attentive listening skills, such as getting the gist of a story, paying attention to beginning sounds, listening for final sounds, etc.

HIGHLIGHTS (LISTENING SKILLS)

- **Listening comprehension skills are closely allied to the other language skills**
- **Youngsters need to be taught how to listen attentively**
- **Listening comprehension can be practiced alone or in conjunction with other language skills**

SPEAKING SKILLS

The goal of most students, including elementary school language students, is to learn how to speak the language in real-life situations, according to Krashen and Terrell (95). The companion skill, of course, is the ability to understand the foreign language. By definition, the speaking skill is the ability of youngsters to use the foreign language in natural situations, within the limits of the content they have been taught. Merely parroting lines of a dialogue (even if the pupil understands fully what she or he is saying) is not a demonstration of proficiency in speaking the foreign language. The youngster needs to be able to use the dialogue with some free variations, and some accuracy of vocabulary, verb forms, idiomatic expressions, etc.

Also among the skills of speaking: the children need to be able to pronounce accurately and have acceptable intonation patterns (phonology). Skills involved in the structure of the language (morphology) and the syntax (word order, negatives, etc.) are important aspects of the skills needed for successful oral communication.

Standard FLES (and FLEX) programs rely, to a great extent, on the following guidelines:

- Speaking in the foreign language should be geared to real-life situations and within the limitations of vocabulary and structure previously taught to the children.

- Errors in pronunciation, structure, word order, etc., are to be expected, since children are urged to use the foreign language as much as possible.

- Vocabulary is taught in context.

- Numerous approaches are possible, such as the dialogue approach, the narrative approach, the question/answer approach, etc.

- There is an interrelationship among the four skills of listening, speaking, reading, and writing. No longer is a minimum waiting period practiced before the printed word is shown.

- There is careful attention paid to sound-letter discrepancies, so that pronunciation remains as accurate and authentic as possible, even after children begin to read the FL.

- The sequence of language skills (first listening, then speaking, then reading, then writing) is largely followed without long delays before the introduction of each skill. Sometimes reading and writing skills are used to enhance listening and speaking skills; sometimes, the other way around. There is less rigidity in the teaching of skills because of their interrelationship.

- Depending on the level and ability of the youngsters, grammar is taught either by modeling or by brief explanation.

- For the most part, the speed of speaking is normal, both by the teacher and the children.

- Utterances may be complete sentences, groups of words, single words, etc., depending upon the nature of the communication activity or situation.
- In order to encourage the children to use the foreign language, English is very limited; only used by the teacher for clarification.
- Whether it is called the direct method, the audiolingual method, or the proficiency method, the best method for FLES and FLEX is involvement in a realistic situation using the foreign language almost exclusively.

Here are some speaking activities:

- Choral and individual repetition of words and phrases
- TPR directions
- Answering questions and asking questions
- Chain drills (*My name is Mary. What is your name?*)
- Describing a picture
- Role-playing a situation (going to a birthday party)
- Playing language games (see Appendix B)
- Welcoming visitors to the classroom
- Introducing people
- Singing songs
- Performing "impromptu card" situations (prepared in advance by the teacher and/or students)
- Telling a story
- Telling about a television program
- Role-playing a television program
- Role-playing the teacher and the class
- Narrating a pantomimed story
- Reciting poems
- Acting out a proverb
- Doing a puppet show
- Dramatizing famous events
- Dramatizing going shopping or eating in a restaurant
- Engaging in conversations about various topics

- Complaining about a poor grade
- Asking questions about a train schedule
- Denying a fight in the school yard
- Insisting on being the leader of the game
- Suggesting that it would be better to play a different game

For additional suggestions on developing the speaking skill through role-playing and dramatics, see the Bibliography: Maley and Duff, 131, 132, 133, 134; and Smith, 187.

Presenting a Dialogue or a Communicative Conversation in FLES and FLEX

I. Introduction

The introduction includes a statement or two about the situation. Pointing to visuals for the characters and the setting, teachers should explain the situation in the foreign language (depending on the age and ability of the youngsters) and in English, if necessary. Obviously, it is preferable to use the foreign language throughout, if possible, without causing too much frustration or anxiety on the part of the children.

II. Presentation

- Go through the entire conversation, pointing to visuals and using motions to convey meaning; ask questions to check understanding.
- Speak at a normal conversational rate; have the students listen carefully.
- Go through the conversation again, and have a full-class response.
- Repeat the conversation with half the class taking one part, and the other half taking the other part.
- Repeat the conversation with boys and girls, rows, or different groups taking each part.

- Present the printed model for the students to read and repeat.
- Have students repeat the teacher's model. (Students should hear other voices, too.)

If it is a real-life situation dialogue, ask the students how they would respond or ask questions. It is essential that students believe that if they were in an environment where the FL is spoken, they could respond in different ways, depending upon the situation and their experience with the language.

Some of the lines in the dialogue suggested by the children may be one-word answers or gestures. This is all right because the approach is to personalize and create natural communication.

Teaching Vocabulary

Vocabulary can be divided into two major categories: passive and active. Passive vocabulary items are those words and phrases that children respond to in listening and in reading. The items are not necessarily taught, but they are modeled in the context of communication. Active vocabulary items are those the children use in their speech and in their writing.

It is to be expected that the youngsters' passive vocabulary will exceed their active vocabulary; that is, the children will be able to understand much more than they will be asked to say; that they will be able to read more than they will be asked to write. These generalizations apply primarily to FLES and FLEX, since children in immersion programs spend so much time with the foreign language that there may not be so large a gap between their active and passive vocabularies.

In teaching vocabulary, teachers should keep certain things in mind.

Vocabulary should be taught in context, never in lists. In the initial presentation of a vocabulary item, it is suggested that teachers give several examples of how the new word can be used. If it is a close cognate, or if it is a false cognate, special attention should be given to both the meaning and the pronunciation.

Many repetitions of vocabulary are necessary, both in the same lesson and in subsequent lessons.

The content is determined by the goals of the program. For example, in a FLEX program, acquisition of an extensive vocabulary is *not* a major goal.

Children should be given *many opportunities to use* vocabulary functionally, in natural situations.

Children should be given opportunities to *interact physically* to help them learn "through their muscles."

Presentation of vocabulary is more effective when *pictures, slides, real objects,* etc., are used. This will help clarify meaning and will minimize the use of English.

Vocabulary is better learned if items are *grouped by themes and situations.*

All kinds of *memory techniques* might be used to help students learn.

Repetition should involve *different modalities of learning* to assist youngsters with different learning styles. Some children, even in the elementary grades, have problems with an approach that uses only listening and speaking. Their preferred style of learning (whether they are aware of it or not) is to use more emphasis on the reading or writing skill. These youngsters are probably the exception in grades K through 4. In grades 5 and 6, more children would show a preference for utilizing both listening and speaking skills along with the reading and writing skills as reinforcement of learning. Teachers should remember that some children learn better through hearing; others through seeing; still others through both hearing and seeing. All children respond well to being given opportunities for interacting physically in some way, which perhaps helps to reinforce the learning. For other suggestions on meeting the needs of individual students, see the Bibliography: Angiolillo, 10; Barnett, 18; Birckbichler and Omaggio, 24; Hunter, 84; and Omaggio, 155.

The Story/Dramatized Technique

Using a story approach from time to time can bring a new excitement to the learning process. The teacher tells a story (usually a folk tale that is rich in the foreign culture), and dramatically teaches vocabulary through actions, gestures, and "props."

Special note: There should be a short refrain that is repeated periodically throughout the story, so that after a while, the children will naturally chime in and repeat the refrain without ever being asked. Such a refrain in Cinderella, for example, might be "She is so sad; she can't go to the ball!"

After the story, the teacher will check comprehension by asking questions. Then, the teacher might divide the story into four or five different sections and assign each section to a different group, so that they will dramatize that part of the story. Vocabulary and key phrases are taught to the class prior to this assignment. Then the assignments might be rotated to different groups, so that each group has an opportunity to work on all the segments of the story. Sometimes (but not always) there is a performance of the story for others to enjoy.

For more gifted language students, the teacher could ask them to change the ending of the story, or change the role of the characters, or see how the story would work in 1987 or in 1604 or in 2015.

For more information about the story approach, see Chapter 5.

The Situation Technique

Various real-life, natural communicative situations can be introduced into the FLES/FLEX/immersion class. They usually are very high in motivational appeal, and children are eager to participate. After motivating students to want to learn the vocabulary and phrases and idiomatic expressions needed for the situation, the teacher then proceeds to present these new items for repetition and practice. Situations could include some of the following:

- Going shopping
- Complaining about something
- Disagreeing about something
- Making up an excuse for some mistake
- Getting angry about something
- Feeling happy about something

- Apologizing for some offense
- Refusing to do something
- Inviting someone to do something
- Commending someone for an accomplishment

After the needed tools of communication have been developed (phrases, vocabulary, idiomatic expressions), the class and the teacher can create a conversation within the framework of the situation or theme. This conversation can then be practiced with partners and in small groups until the students are ready to try the conversation aloud. Later on, small groups of children will meet to find ways to vary the situation according to their own creative talents, using the dictionary and with the assistance of the teacher. These alternate situations can now be presented to the class.

For more information about using situations, see Chapter 5.

HIGHLIGHTS (SPEAKING SKILLS)

- **Speaking is interrelated to the other language skills**
- **Speaking is communication in real-life situations**
- **Various approaches can promote speaking proficiency: dialogue, story, skit, situation**

READING SKILLS

Reading in traditional FLES programs consisted of reading labels, captions, and two- to three-line paragraphs geared to what the students were able to comprehend and say in the foreign language.

Today, that might be appropriate for FLEX programs that have limited time constraints, limited goals, and a limited range of content to be covered during the FLEX sessions.

FLES programs and immersion programs, on the other hand, have a broader scope for all language skills, including reading. The content of the program will raise students' sights to the degree that they will attempt to read for meaning materials with both familiar and unfamiliar words and phrases. They will be taught many of the language arts skills of understanding through context, picture cues, reading between the lines, guessing, skimming, and other skills. Reading materials will provide a challenge to able students who can utilize higher-order cognitive thinking skills in their attempts to get meaning from the printed page.

In grades 1 and 2, reading readiness consists of labeling objects around the classroom, using familiar vocabulary and structures; labeling pictures, charts, and maps; and writing the date, weather, and attendance, as well as appropriate holiday sayings. Developing experience charts are appropriate for this level.

In grade 3 and above (or earlier, depending on the class), reading will consist of experience charts (material dictated by the students and written by the teacher on a large chart). The advantages of using an experience chart are many, particularly since the students are encouraged to speak about what they have experienced (and learned). There is a controversy about whether the teacher records statements made by the children, including errors, or whether the teacher takes the essential thought and writes it down correctly in the foreign language. It is my opinion that students should not be presented with incorrect patterns in the foreign language, and therefore I favor recording the *ideas*, but recording them correctly.

Use of the flannelboard, flashcards, overhead transparencies, the computer, and many other devices is appropriate, too. Some of the steps in teaching reading might include:

- Teacher motivates the material by creating interest and presenting vocabulary.
- Teacher reads material a paragraph at a time, asking questions to check comprehension.
- Teacher uses sentence strips (in order, then out of order).
- Teacher uses phonics and other word-attack skills to help students deal with sound-letter discrepancies.
- Questions will help students frame key phrases.
- More sophisticated questions will help students learn how to make inferences from the reading materials.

- Carefully composed questions will help students develop critical thinking skills (see Wasserman, 215).

- Challenges for some students in learning skills of comparing, describing similarities and differences, categorizing, etc., help in developing higher-order thinking skills (see Sternberg, 197).

- Teacher elicits summary of the materials in logical order of sequence.

- Teacher will ask children to role-play or dramatize the material, if appropriate.

- Teacher may ask students to reinforce the reading with writing (depending on the goals of the program and the class).

An important aspect of the reading process is learning how to use a dictionary. Once this skill is learned, the more able students will be able to read many varied materials independently, for the most part. Various components of dictionary use will be presented over a series of lessons, with particular emphasis upon the pronunciation keys. This is particularly true for immersion.

It should be remembered that word analysis, sound-symbol analysis, phonics, generalizations for word-attack skills, and correct pronunciation will often be fused during any given lesson.

Finally, teachers will note wide differences in the range of reading abilities in the foreign language, and will make provision for them by providing suitable materials, partner practice, and group work, which will reinforce learning. By following the developmental steps of (1) reading readiness, (2) reading familiar materials, (3) reading recombined materials, (4) controlled text reading with comprehension checks, and (5) for some students, independent reading, teachers will be able to incorporate a variety of reading strategies in planning foreign language lessons.

In recent years, reading activities have been correlated with audio and visual supports, such as cassette recordings and video presentations. These, too, help students gain independence in reading and broaden their cognitive skills.

For additional information about teaching reading skills in second-language programs, see the Bibliography: Allen, 4; and Genesee, 68.

Here are some reading activities:

- Reading aloud in chorus or individually
- Completing a sentence when a choice is given
- Reading to solve a riddle
- Choosing related items in a list of related and unrelated items
- Answering questions based on a short paragraph
- Making inferences based on a short paragraph
- Reading letters written by classmates
- Reading directions and following them (e.g., *Go to the door and open it*)
- Reading two advertisements and comparing prices
- Reading six sentences about a story and putting them in the correct order
- Reading and understanding definitions in the dictionary (on their level)
- Reading the homework assignment on the chalkboard
- Reading a foreign language magazine
- Reading a comic strip in the foreign language
- Reading a menu and making a decision on what to order
- Reading the television schedule and deciding what to watch
- Reading a letter from a pen pal

HIGHLIGHTS (READING SKILLS)

- **Reading skills are interrelated with the other language skills**

- **Reading readiness activities and word-attack skills help to get meaning from the printed page**

- **The key steps in reading skills development are: reading readiness, reading familiar materials, reading recombined materials, controlled reading/ comprehension checks, and independent reading**

WRITING SKILLS

It should be noted that reading and writing skills are closely related. In fact, research indicates that there is an interrelationship among all the skills of listening, speaking, reading, and writing (Krashen and Terrell, 95). Speaking and writing are considered to be the active production skills; listening and reading are thought to be the passive skills, sources of comprehensible input.

In FLEX programs (those where limited time is devoted to foreign language instruction), writing activities are limited to brief captions, labels and simple sentences, greeting cards, and informal notes to friends and family. The writing activities are functional in nature.

In sequential FLES programs, writing skills are developed in somewhat greater depth, and students are encouraged to keep a student notebook or perform some of the functional writing activities that follow, although it is helpful if the teacher presents the materials through listening and speaking skills and extended practice. No longer are second-language specialists advocating a strict adherence to the learning sequence mandated by the audiolingual movement, such as listening first, then speaking, then reading, then writing.

In immersion programs, writing skills cover the content areas as well as spelling, accents, punctuation, structure, etc., in the language of instruction. The writing skills are developed as a direct outgrowth of the content-area instruction, and thus reinforce not only the foreign language, but the other concepts required by the content areas. In addition, writing skills in English are developed.

Some of the early beginning writing skills might include the following activities: copying, matching and copying, spot dictation, and word jumbles.

Sample Word Puzzles (Spanish)

WORD JUMBLES (Parts of the Body)

CABO	ZIRAN
RODOL	NEDITE
PRUCEO	NOMA

COPYING

A Q U I   E S T Á   U N   S O M B R E R O

_ _ _ _   _ _ _ _   _ _   _ _ _ _ _ _ _

SPOT DICTATION

1. Hoy es _____ .
2. ¿Tienes un _____ ?
3. ¿Dońde está la _____ ?
4. ¿_____ es?
5. _____ amigos.

MATCHING AND COPYING

la leche	es rojo _____
la mantequilla	es blanca _____
el café	es amarilla _____
el vino	es negro _____

It should be noted here that the sound-symbol analysis described in reading skills might be continued in the development of writing skills.

More advanced writing skills would be writing for specific, functional purposes, such as the following:

Writing Skills Activities for FLES, FLEX, Immersion

*Ideas for a Student Notebook**

Students will write about:

- Self-identification—pictures of things the student likes to do, eat, wear, etc.
- Family identification
- News events at home, at school, etc.
- Places student visits
- Friends (similar to self-identification)
- Pet or pets
- Favorite TV program and stars
- Favorite movie stars
- Favorite sports people
- Favorite hobbies
- Holidays student likes—contrasted with student in foreign culture
- Celebrating the student's birthday

---

*Depending on the grade level, experience with the foreign language, and ability of the students in FLES or FLEX. Students in immersion will be able to keep more sophisticated notebooks on these and other topics.

- Favorite books
- Favorite magazines
- Favorite occupation(s)
- Cartoon(s) and captions
- Favorite recipes
- Favorite telephone numbers and pictures of friends/relatives
- Directions to student's home, with pictures
- Résumé for a neighborhood job
- Poems
- Greeting cards for special occasions
- Calendar of events at home and/or at school
- Invitations to a special event
- Puzzles
- Riddles
- Simulated passport

Note: Class newspaper could be a compilation of short items from all youngsters.

Other writing activities consist of multiple choice, true or false, matching, more complex exercises, transformation (affirmative to negative and/or interrogative), completions, etc. **Note:** It is almost impossible to separate writing activities from reading activities, and this being the case, the teacher may wish to reinforce one of the skills with the other and vice-versa.

A final word about dictation. It is a writing activity, and a worthwhile one. However, it is not solely a writing activity. Many teachers feel that it is a combination of listening comprehension, reading, and writing, and probably some silent speaking, as well. It is useful to use dictation at the completion of a topic, unit, or any segment of learning. It can be used for testing, but it is extremely useful as a diagnostic tool for the teacher to determine what needs reteaching, who needs special assistance, and what the specific problems are. A dictation given two days in succession will also be very helpful. At the early stages of writing, the use of a spot dictation is advisable. This consists of having students write one or two words in the context of sentences or a short paragraph. An example of a spot dictation follows:

> Students complete the missing word or words as the teacher dictates them while reading the complete sentence.
>
> 1. Il fait _____ aujourd'hui.
> 2. C'est aujourd'hui _____, le _____ avril.

In the first sentence, students are to fill in *beau*, for example, as the teacher reads the complete sentence aloud. In the second sentence, students are to fill in *mardi* and *sept*, for example, as the teacher reads the complete sentence aloud.

Students then correct their papers (or turn them in to be corrected by the teacher). If students correct their own papers, teachers must check carefully, as correcting (and proofreading skills) must be developed over a period of time. During an oral discussion with the students, the teacher might use this as an opportunity to point out sound-letter discrepancies in the foreign language.

Writing, then, should not be stressed over other skills. Writing for different purposes can be developed at both early and later stages of FLES and Immersion. Casual writing (a note to a friend) should be comprehensible, while more formal writing (a letter to the teacher and/or principal) should be comprehensible and thoroughly correct. Still, writing is one of the skills which should be developed along with the other skills, with the primary goal of communication. Depending on the age of the learner, teachers will find that some students need the support of reading and writing in order to understand and speak. Fifth and sixth graders are probably more dependent on reading and writing than students in earlier grades. Thus, in developing writing skills, the purpose, age, and individual student learning styles should be taken into consideration.

Sample Reading and Writing Activity for FLES and FLEX, Grades 2–4

J'ai faim

——J'ai faim. Qu'est-ce qu'on mange?
——Le dindon.
——Mm, j'aime le dindon. Et quoi encore?
——Les légumes: les pommes de terre et les haricots verts.
——Et le dessert?
——Le gâteau et la glace.
——Oh, c'est délicieux!

le pain	le fruit	le dindon	le poulet
la pomme	la poire	les raisins	les fraises
le poisson	le gâteau	la glace	le dessert

Le Menu:

_____

_____

_____

_____

_____

Note: for developing higher-order thinking skills, ask the students to describe similarities and differences between a pear and an apple, for example.

Sample Thematic Worksheet for FLES and Immersion Reading and Writing

El avión

Vocabulary:

el anuncio	la compañía de aviación
el pilota	despegar
el avión	aterrizar
la pista	el vuelo
la salida	la puerta
el cinturón de seguridad	los billetes sencillos
el aeropuerto	los billetes de ida y vuelta
los pasajeros	las maletas
el equipaje	el clima

Anuncios

La compañía _____ anuncia el _____ de su
_____ 201 destino Caracas. Los pasajeros pasan por la
_____ número 30. En el avión los pasajeros se abrocharán
el _____ __ _____. El avión irá a la _____ y
_____ . Muchas gracias y buen viaje.

La Conversación entre dos pasajeros:

El hombre: _____

La mujer: _____

El hombre: _____

La mujer: _____

El hombre: _____

La mujer: _____

La Geografía:

¿Dónde está Caracas?

¿Cuál es la capital del Perú?
¿Quién es el presidente de Méjico?

HIGHLIGHTS (WRITING SKILLS)

- **Writing is interrelated with the other language skills**
- **Writing is communication in real-life situations**
- **Writing should not be stressed over other skills**
- **Writing for natural purposes should be the objective**

CULTURAL AWARENESS ASPECTS OF FLES/FLEX/IMMERSION

The content of cultural aspects is a vital segment of a FLES/FLEX/immersion program. Language is a function of culture, and as such reflects the culture of the areas where the foreign language is spoken. Youngsters are fascinated by what youngsters their age do in the foreign culture—how it is similar, how it is different from the ways we know in American culture. As Larew (103) puts it: "The youngsters want to know how the Spanish-speaking people live and work; what they eat, dream, feel." Teaching these cultural components is not the memorization of isolated facts and figures. Rather, it is an attempt to help children understand a different way of life, using another language of communication. Language, intonation, gestures all convey some aspects of the foreign culture.

Cultural awareness at the elementary school level is *not*:

- "Flag-waving"
- Facts to be memorized
- Stereotypes
- Generalities
- Based on outmoded concepts

- Only the unfamiliar and the differences
- Isolated concepts
- Any other procedures that do not promote greater understanding

Language *is* culture. Some examples are the use of *tu* and *vous* in French, intonation, gestures, songs, emotional exclamations, and so forth. Teachers will find many activities to integrate cultural components with linguistic aspects, and in general terms here are a number of suggestions:

1. Media presentations (pictures, slides, video, film, etc.)
2. Current events in the FL-speaking country (countries)
3. Trips and excursions to neighborhood displays, restaurants, landmarks in the community, bookshops, etc.
4. Traveling exhibits that can be obtained for the classroom
5. Guest speakers (*Note:* In preparation for a visit, speakers will be grateful if children list questions in advance.)
6. Displays set up by the school and/or neighborhood specialist
7. Playing authentic games with the children
8. Dancing authentic folk dances
9. Singing authentic songs
10. Learning and understanding authentic proverbs
11. Having a pen pal from the foreign culture
12. Examining realia from the foreign culture
13. Recognizing famous places in the foreign culture
14. Learning how to look at maps
15. Learning how to recognize street signs
16. Contrasting the appearance of public servants (e.g., police in Germany *vs.* U.S.)
17. Reading nonfiction books about the foreign culture
18. Looking through travel brochures and discussing them
19. Reading fiction books about the foreign culture in English (Immersion students, however, can do this in the foreign language.)

20. Contrasting meals, schools, homes, leisure activities
21. Discussing stereotypes reported in the media
22. Identifying "national characteristics," if any
23. Contrasting the concepts of time
24. Contrasting family relationships
25. Contrasting attitudes toward age
26. Discovering what the "new words" are in the foreign culture
27. Understanding nonverbal communication in the foreign culture
28. Understanding the influence of weather and geographical location on the foreign culture
29. Researching the country's heroes (and heroines)
30. What are the important holidays? How are they observed?
31. What kind of money is used in the foreign culture? Does it reflect the culture?
32. What is the mealtime schedule?
33. What are the favorite foods? Which foods are taboo?
34. What kind of schools do they have? How much homework do the children get?
35. Have things changed in the last five years? Why?

Teachers and youngsters could most certainly continue this list from the questions the children ask and what is currently happening in the foreign culture(s). Where a language is spoken in several different countries, it would be necessary for the children to understand that the Spanish spoken in Argentina is slightly different from the Spanish spoken in Venezuela, for example. Advertisements in the newspapers, magazines, and street signs give additional clues to the foreign culture.

Teachers, then, should not set aside ten minutes Friday afternoons to "teach" culture, but will be alert for the opportunities during the language lessons to present cultural components, urge the children to research and explore, display, encourage, explain—in short, make the cultural component an integral part of language learning.

On those few occasions when teachers wish to highlight differences and/or similarities, they may try some of the following procedures:

Cultural assimilators. A cross-cultural situation is stopped at a given point and the children are asked to select from a list of three or four possibilities the one choice they think would fit or follow the given situation. The most important part of this activity is the discussion of why one possibility is appropriate but the other one is not.

Culture capsule. Cross-cultural listing of a unit describing the foreign culture and American culture (descriptions of various aspects of the culture).

Psychomotor unit or theme. Statements and actions demonstrating how an important activity in the foreign culture would be conducted and how it is conducted in the U.S. (e.g., going on a picnic, bringing different types of food, etc.).

TPR. Giving directions for actions in the foreign culture as contrasted with those for the U.S. culture (e.g., going shopping; first going to the butcher, then the grocery, etc., as contrasted with going to the supermarket in the U.S.). **Note:** determine if in the last few years there are supermarkets in the foreign culture.

Using vocabulary to contrast different cultures. For example, using the words "home" or "house" and showing how people in the foreign culture have a different conceptual meaning for these words as contrasted with Americans.

Using activities and experiences with the foreign language, children can gain an insight into similar and dissimilar cultural patterns. Cultural concepts can be brought into the language lesson incidentally (such as different ways of shaking hands in greeting someone) or as a specific teaching concept, such as when to use the familiar and the formal "you" in the foreign language. Everyday topics are essential: food, dress, homes, dance, toys, family life, art, music, time, stories, folk tales, customs, sports, leisure activities, famous personalities, holidays, word derivations, etc.

For additional suggestions on the teaching of culture, see Bourque and Chehy, 25; Damen, 37; Donoghue, 47; Griffin, 76; Joiner, 89; Seelye, 182; and Sparkman, 190.

HIGHLIGHTS

- Language *is* culture
- Cross-cultural understanding involves similarities and differences
- Stereotypes are to be avoided!

VII

Methods of Teaching Foreign Languages in the Elementary School

Because the goals of standard FLES and FLEX are limited with respect to the linguistic and cultural goals, this section will provide an overview of methods of teaching standard FLES and FLEX, with special adaptations when FLES is sequential and occurs frequently (3 to 5 times per week). Immersion methods will be discussed separately, since the focus is not primarily on acquisition of language, but using language as the tool of instruction in the basic skills of the elementary school curriculum.

GENERAL GUIDELINES FOR FLES AND FLEX

1. Words and expressions are taught in context, not in isolation.
2. Emphasis is on the four skills of language learning: listening, speaking, reading, and writing. These are the "bread and butter" skills.
3. Associations are made between the foreign language and the object, action, or concept, rather than with the English equivalent.
4. English is used sparingly, when necessary. However, sometimes a brief explanation in English may save time and avoid confusion.
5. A wide range of materials of instruction is recommended.
6. Emphasis is on functional communication activities in real-life situations.

7. Grammatical structure is learned by imitation, repetition, and sometimes analogy.

8. Each lesson requires a great deal of systematic review, re-entry, and reinforcement.

9. The pace of the lesson is lively and is maintained by well-timed changes from one activity to another.

10. The cultural component is interwoven with the linguistic activities.

11. The children are encouraged to speak to one another in the foreign language about topics of interest to them, within the constraints of vocabulary and structure.

12. In addition to being taught correct pronunciation, the pupils are taught intonation in context, with meaning.

13. Although both children and teachers recognize that they are engaged in a serious study of the foreign language, the teacher capitalizes on interest appeal and humor to enhance the learning.

14. Evaluation is an ongoing and integral part of the teaching and learning process.

15. Since children cannot sit quietly for long periods of time, action and motion are important components of successful lessons.

FLES Note

Since more time for FLES is assumed, more emphasis can be included on reading and writing skills, along with the listening and speaking skills.

GUIDELINES FOR IMMERSION

1. The foreign language is used throughout the day in immersion programs; at least 50 percent of the day for partial immersion programs.

2. All instructions are in the foreign language and children are

expected to respond in the foreign language, although some children use English for a short time.

3. By the end of the first year, children usually understand almost everything, except for presentations of new work and vocabulary.

4. The teaching of reading in the foreign language parallels the methods used in other schools for the teaching of reading in English. For some languages like French, extra attention has to be paid to sound–letter discrepancies.

5. Math and science have manipulative practice, which reinforces the new vocabulary.

6. Language arts is taught from the point of view of the foreign language.

7. The foreign language is not taught; it is the medium of instruction.

8. Children learn how to understand, speak, read, and write, as they study all aspects of the elementary school curriculum.

For specific information about teaching subjects of the elementary school curriculum (in partial and total immersion programs), consult elementary school texts such as Seefeldt and Barbour, 181; and Sheperd and Ragan, 184. For additional information on methodology in immersion programs, see the Bibliography: Anderson and Rhodes, 6; Curtain, 36; De Lorenzo and Gladstein, 40; Derrick and Khorshed, 41; Genesee, 68, 69, 70; Howe, 83; Jacobs, 86; Krashen, 94; Lundin and Dolson, 128; McLaughlin, 136; Met, 141; and Ozete, 158.

OVERVIEW OF METHODOLOGY IN FLES AND FLEX

- An informal approach, with an emphasis on comprehension and speaking the language
- Choral and group repetition
- Individual repetition
- Listening activities (listening to the teacher, to recorded voices, to dialogues, poems, stories, questions)

- Singing songs
- Reading labels around the room
- Reading simple sentences
- Writing simple sentences and labels
- Writing letters and invitations
- Reciting dialogues, songs, poems
- Preparing skits and dramatizations
- Learning about different ways of living
- Learning about holidays in different cultures
- Learning about folk tales in different cultures
- Integrating language with different subjects in the curriculum, such as music, art, science, etc.
- Enriching and expanding knowledge about different subjects in the curriculum as they relate to the language being studied

CLASSROOM ENVIRONMENT

The ambiance of the classroom is conducive to effective teaching and learning. If the decorations are interesting and attractive and are used as aids to the teaching/learning process, learning is enhanced. Posters, pictures, dolls, collages, streamers, charts, maps, costumes, menus, flashcards, etc., help to make an appealing environment of the place(s) where the foreign language is spoken. Sometimes, in the elementary school classroom, it can be little more than a "corner" with a bulletin board. Sometimes it can be a foreign language area, shared by different grades. In all cases, however, it should be changed frequently, and items on display can be used in developing stories, dialogues, and real-life situations. Samples of children's work are particularly effective for encouraging students and for sharing their work with other students, parents, administrators, etc.

Another aspect of the classroom environment has to do with the seating arrangement of the students. For some lessons, the teacher will want to have a full-class environment. On other occasions, when the teacher wishes to have partner practice, the youngsters can be seated by twos. Other times, there will be small groups of four or five, for specific purposes of rehearsing a dialogue, doing research together, planning scenery for a dramatization, etc. If the school has equipped the foreign language area with a listening corner, a group of three or four may be listening to a cassette tape or language master cards with headsets. Others may be working on a computer program.

Other essential components of the foreign language classroom may include:

- A picture file of the important topics (food, clothing, etc.)
- A clothing box with different articles of clothing
- Records, cassettes
- Tapes
- Books and magazines (appropriate for this level)
- Foreign language newspapers
- Flags
- A transparency file based on the topics (food, clothing, etc.)
- A professions box with hats for all types of professions
- Other "props" for situations and communications

The most important aspect of the classroom environment has to do with helping students to feel at ease, comfortable yet challenged by interesting activities. The teacher's manner should be friendly, encouraging, and helpful, so as to minimize any anxiety on the part of the children. Some teachers start the lesson with music (culturally authentic, of course!). Other teachers have a special hat (sombrero?) or special puppet who speaks only the foreign language. If the children are entering the classroom from another room, the teacher is there to greet them and comment in a friendly fashion about individual student's interests. During the lesson, a change-of-pace activity is a "must" (usually one involving movement). This usually consists of some movement or repetition of familiar material. This tends to reduce the anxiety level, and the children are then ready to engage in other activities related to the lesson. Humor is also an important aspect of the classroom environment, although it should never be at the expense of any of the students. Finally, an element of surprise in a lesson (a funny TPR activity such as "Put the pencil on your friend's head," or a new puppet or a cartoon about snow in June) can capture the children's interest. When children learn to expect that there will be such surprises, when they understand that laughter can be incorporated into the classwork, they will enjoy the process of language learning as well as the results. They will also enjoy making suggestions.

Another way to encourage students is to praise their efforts. "Très bien," "excelente," and "wunderbar" are helpful, except when teachers fall into a pattern of praising every response with the same brush (or same expressions). Students quickly learn that there will be no differentiation between praise for an ordinary response to a review warmup question and praise for a response using a new concept. Then, too, the student who volunteers a question or response (never having done so before) merits unusual praise. I recently came across a list of 88 different ways to give praise in English! Surely FLES/FLEX/immersion teachers can develop 10 or 12 or more expressions that can be interspersed judiciously so that they convey real appreciation and real encouragement.

Don't hesitate to tell them when they are wonderful, fantastic, extraordinary, unbelievably good, going in the right direction, great, really getting it, trying very hard, stupendous, marvelous, spectacular, tremendous, terrific, beyond your wildest dreams!

For additional suggestions on reducing anxiety in the classroom, see the Bibliography: Everything, 56.

REPETITION AND THE NEED TO STIMULATE CREATIVE LANGUAGE

Whether repetition is used for developing comprehension or as a model for students to imitate, it is an extremely important component of teaching foreign languages to young children. In FLES and FLEX, it is crucial. In immersion programs, since language is the means of communication and instruction, the sheer volume of language provides a broad base for learning both the language and the content areas. Still, repetition plays a role in immersion programs, since not all students in immersion programs have the same ability for learning.

In FLES and FLEX, care must be taken to vary the types of repetition, even of the same content. This can be accomplished by changing some elements in the materials, by changing some visuals (pictures changed to transparencies, for example), by changing the manner in which something is repeated (softly, loudly, boys only, girls only, etc.), by changing hand signals, by having students record the content, and many other ways. The key word is *variety*. Someone once commented that the way to teach foreign language to children was the "What's the color of George Washington's gray horse?" approach. This implies that students need to *hear* and comprehend the language before they are able to produce it. They cannot make it up out of thin air! Thus, if a teacher held up a picture of a gray horse, he or she first would have to teach the word for *horse*, then the color *gray*, then possession showing that this was George Washington's gray horse before asking the question "What's the color of George Washington's horse?" This process of teaching the new vocabulary and structures would take a number of repetitions on the part of the teacher and the students.

But if teachers continue to repeat the same thing over and over again, boredom becomes the unwelcome visitor to the classroom. Every language teacher wrestles with this problem, and here are a few suggestions for stimulating creative language activities:

Use a variety of materials, such as pictures, signs, key words, sequence materials (arranging pictures and/or words of a story in sequence), TV schedules, advertisements, stuffed animals, labels on food and other items, photographs, sounds, videos, transparencies, etc.

Personalize the language concepts in order to give students many different opportunities to express their ideas, thoughts, and feelings, such as:

"I am happiest when _____"
"I would like to be _____"
"My friends can be sure that I will _____"

"If I had a million dollars, I would _____"

"Right now I am thinking _____"

"I hate _____"

"I get angry when _____"

Change the activity when the children get restless (probably after ten minutes at the most!). Using a TPR activity tends to ease the tension.

Include change-of-pace activities, which need not depart drastically from the goals of the lesson. For example, when practicing numbers, they could be practiced counting backwards, by twos, using arithmetical operations, bouncing a ball, throwing a beanbag, giving dates of birthdays of members of the class and of famous people, etc.

Include songs, which in addition to providing a pleasurable change of pace, help to reinforce pronunciation, structures, and vocabulary.

Plan games that help to teach, review, and reinforce language skills and provide a change of pace during the lesson. Some simple games, requiring little preparation, include numbers to be guessed, Simon Says, Reverse Simon Says (see Games in Appendix B), "Guess whose voice it is," "Guess who has the picture of the dog?" and others.

Have students role-play, from time to time, the part of the teacher for a short segment of the lesson. The things you will observe about yourself! Your voice, your gestures . . .

Use partner-practice once in a while to reinforce the learning.

One should always be on the lookout for opportunities that will help develop higher cognitive skills, while still reviewing vocabulary and expressions. Asking children to comment on the differences and similarities of a horse and a dog, for example, can not only reinforce the vocabulary, but can stimulate higher levels of thinking skills. Showing pictures of different animals, for example, can reinforce the vocabulary. However, going a step further and asking children to categorize the various animals (those with four feet, those with two feet, etc.) will add a more sophisticated dimension to the language lessons and will integrate them with the skills development program of the entire elementary school curriculum.

Another way to encourage creative ideas on the part of the children is to have them listen to a tape with different sounds on it (some familiar sounds, some unfamiliar). Then, children can be encouraged to describe what they think they are hearing or to invent an event, a dialogue, a narrative, etc., about these sounds.

For additional suggestions on developing creative language skills, see the Bibliography: Landry, 100, 101; Maley and Duff, 132, 133, 134; and Stanislawczyk and Yavner, 192.

TIPS FOR THE NEW TEACHER OF FLES OR FLEX (OR HOW TO GET SOME CLASSROOM "MAGIC")

1. Look forward to teaching the language and have the children look forward to learning another language.
2. Introduce yourself in the foreign language. Use a special hat, demonstrate on a map where people speak the language.
3. Bring a puppet (a sock puppet might do) and introduce it in the foreign language.
4. Bring a calendar with the month in the foreign language.
5. Have students keep a foreign language notebook to keep pictures, calendars, illustrated activities, weather charts, etc.
6. Think of a number of things to do in any one lesson, however short. Have students repeat words and use motions, listen, read to the children, dramatize and role-play, sing, dance, illustrate, copy a short sentence, make greeting cards, etc. These are the types of activities to choose from.
7. Do not become discouraged if the children do not remember too well from lesson to lesson. It takes a lot of practice and a lot of review, and a lot of patience on your part.
8. Always try to have a surprise for the children, such as something in a box for a guessing game, which is a good review of vocabulary previously taught.
9. Make sure that the children learn something new in every lesson, as well as review other items that had been presented previously.

10. Develop a set of hand motions to guide the children:
    - when to listen
    - when to repeat
    - when to answer as a whole class, as a row, or as a group
    - when to imitate certain motions
11. End the lesson with a hint of what will be happening in the next lesson.
12. Use a variety of materials: pictures, charts, real objects, toys, hats, puppets, and all kinds of records, tapes, videos, etc.
13. Use as a guide in planning: "something old and something new."
14. Try to have children listen to a variety of voices: male, female, young, old.
15. Use as many different reading materials as possible: magazines, readers, newspapers, poems, comic books, cartoons, etc.
16. Appeal to children's individual preferences and interests. Give them opportunities to express them while learning, such as starting a statement and having students complete it in different ways. For example, "Summer makes me feel _____."
17. Move around—have students move around.
18. Try to build a lesson around the four skills and culture.
19. Give individual children an opportunity to conduct a game.
20. Remember—the goal is *communication*!

PLANNING LESSONS

What are some of the essential components of a FLES or FLEX lesson?

- Warmup using familiar material
- Periodic review and reteaching
- New work or new presentation based on a functional situation
- Song, game, change of pace
- Pupil-to-pupil conversations and partner practice

- Variety of materials
- Informal, nonthreatening environment
- TPR or motion activities
- Variety of lesson formats
- Some form of summary of new work
- Evaluation (not necessarily testing) of what was actually learned
- Plans for next lesson
- Followup activities
- Some form of cultural component included
- All four skills included (listening, speaking, reading, writing) if appropriate to the class
- Evidence that the lesson is pleasurable for teacher and students

Suggested Lesson Plan Format

Lesson	Time
1. Warmup (familiar material) Greetings, health, weather, numbers, colors, etc.	3–5 minutes
2. New material (include culture) Dialogue, song, drill, poem, narrative, etc.	7–10 minutes
3. Change of pace (song, TPR, etc.)	2–3 minutes
4. Review of previous material (use a checklist)	8–10 minutes
5. Reading and writing	8–10 minutes
6. Summary and plans for followup	2–4 minutes

Notes:

1. This type of lesson plan could be adapted for use in a 15 to 45 minute lesson.

2. Each segment could be changed to fit the special needs of the class.

3. Attractive visuals (and listening materials) will enhance each of the segments.

4. Movement activities at this level are a **must**. These could be included in at least one of the segments, particularly the change of activity.

5. Situations, rather than topics, can be written into the long- and short-range plans.

6. This plan can be used in a daily, sequential program as well as in a brief once-a-week schedule.

For sample lesson plans, see Appendix A.

FOLLOWUP AND REINFORCEMENT OF LEARNING

Teachers find that much better results are obtained when there is some provision for followup and reinforcement of learning. Whether it is called homework or extra-credit work or out-of-school games or assignments, it is still helpful for children to have many opportunities to practice the language in meaningful situations for them.

Here are some ideas on various ways to reinforce the learning:

1. Encourage children to find pictures to illustrate what they have learned and to keep picture dictionaries.

2. Have children make a calendar for the month (or longer) to illustrate some of their activities at home and at school.

3. Assign children to find "foreign" words in newspaper articles, magazines, advertisements, etc.

4. Have children make a family tree, labeling each person in the foreign language. They might use actual photographs of family members. They could make a booklet entitled "Me."

5. Ask the children to practice a dialogue with a relative or friend.

6. Have the children teach vocabulary or a dialogue to someone else.

7. Encourage children to bring in favorite toys that can be used in adapting a dialogue.

8. Have children bring in materials (objects or artwork or written projects) for a bulletin-board display. A child-made map or diorama is useful, too.

9. Ask the children to bring in materials made in a foreign country for a "realia" cultural display.

10. Assign children to write letters to their pen pals and bring in materials to be sent to a class pen pal in a foreign country.

11. Develop a class foreign language newspaper with student contributions of articles, cartoons, drawings, etc.

12. Have children make greeting cards for their friends and families.

13. Ask the children to keep a weather record in the foreign language in various places, thus practicing dates, months of the year, days of the week, and weather expressions.

14. Have children listen to recordings in the foreign language (perhaps a fairy tale recorded by the teacher or a native speaker).

15. Encourage the children to create their own "restaurant" with its special menus for different days of the week.

16. Have children create a game based on a class lesson, such as a game to practice colors, numbers, etc. In this category they would also create a follow-the-dots puzzle to practice numbers and the name of the object.

17. Have the children make up riddles in the foreign language to try to "stump" their classmates.

18. Ask the children to think up different types of TPR activities, especially the humorous or surprising ones.

19. Have the children think of different ways to end a familiar story.

20. Ask the children to think about "What if" situations, such as: "What if the Eiffel Tower were in Chicago?"

MOTIVATION OF STUDENTS FOR LEARNING

For every activity in school or in life, there must be motivation. Even at the FLES/FLEX/immersion level, the teacher should be cognizant of the need to find different ways to interest the children in the concepts being addressed. There is a phenomenon identified as the "four-minute barrier"—a short time during which contacts are established, affirmed, or rejected.

If we think of this barrier in terms of the daily lesson, we should examine what teachers do during the first four minutes of class. Does the teacher, for example, check attendance, homework, distribute papers or books? Is there a repetitive or a predictable manner in the way teachers begin each lesson? True, sometimes it is comforting to students to know what to expect. On the other hand, do teachers plan something different for those first four minutes, something to establish a motivation for learning? Why not arouse curiosity, why not set the stage for learning, why not excite the thirst for knowledge, why not rivet students' attention upon what is to follow? How to do this? Consider some of the following:

- Showing a short film (3–5 minutes)
- Singing a song
- Having the teacher or a student dressed as a famous historical figure
- Having the students guess what is in a mystery box
- Writing a secret message on the board in the foreign language
- Pantomiming a message
- Repeating a future date each day for two weeks concerning an undisclosed event on that date
- Unrolling a new poster
- Bringing a new puppet
- Posting a new banner
- Reading a short paragraph in the foreign language and stopping at a crucial point

These strategies and many, many others can help motivate students for learning and make the "four-minute barrier" an important segment of the effective lesson.

Is it possible to identify the various components of successful classroom motivation? Here are a few guide questions:

- Is the teacher's personality encouraging?
- Does the teacher have a sense of humor?
- Is there a brisk pace and variety of activities?
- Is the content of sufficient challenge and interest to the students?
- Is there enrichment for some students and attention to the needs of others?
- And finally . . . Did they learn something today, and do they *want* to come back for more?

TOTAL PHYSICAL RESPONSE APPROACH (TPR)

Experience and research supports the thesis that children learn through physical motions. Seefeldt and Barbour (181) state that "children learn through their senses including their muscles." Children like to learn with all kinds of motion, with moving around, with pantomime as well as words. They cannot sit quietly for long periods of time, and need frequent changes of activities. Obviously, the attention span will be longer as children get older and mature, but even sixth graders are not able to sustain attention to language learning for more than ten minutes at a time for a particular segment of the lesson. That is why the recommended lesson plan contains many short segments.

The following is an example of a TPR activity suitable for a FLES or FLEX class, using standard FLES/FLEX methodology:

Levez-vous.   Je me lève.
Allez à la porte.   Je vais à la porte.
Frappez à la porte.   Je frappe à la porte.
Ouvrez la porte.   J'ouvre la porte.
Fermez la porte.   Je ferme la porte.

After listening to the commands and performing the actions, the children will repeat both the commands and the responses, using appropriate actions with their fingers and hands. Then several children will say the words and move to and from the door. Using the "comprehensible input" approach, the commands, the responses, and the actions will be modeled by the teacher and the motions modeled by the children, without production or speaking. If the time for listening and understanding is sufficient, many of the children will have learned both the commands and the responses (including the motions) with ease. The teacher must be alert for those with special needs and special learning styles who will need additional assistance, perhaps in the form of drills and group work.

Therefore, when teachers plan their lessons, in addition to including content and the various components suggested, they should also include materials needed and TPR activities.

Other TPR activities for FLES and FLEX, and often as a change of pace for immersion classes, are

- Playing all kinds of games to provide opportunities for movement

- Using visual aids can be incorporated into TPR activities: students are asked to place them in various parts of the room, on top of desks, etc.

- Balls, balloons, flashcards, and toys can all be "props" in moving-around-the-room activities, in response to commands. These would also include counting and clapping activities.

- Dramatizing familiar stories (fairy tales or TV programs) is appropriate. For example, Guignol puppets in French offer very strong TPR possibilities, with their characteristic punching and hitting activities.

- Role-playing familiar daily activities contains many motion activities, such as stretching upon awakening, brushing teeth and hair, getting dressed, eating breakfast, etc. Other activities could include going to the doctor, going to the supermarket, going to the restaurant, etc.

- Using props of all kinds, such as clothing, table settings, hats, to denote different occupations, puppets, tools, etc.
- Jazzercising and other physical exercise patterns to establish the rhythms of the language
- Playing games, such as relay races, to focus on the vocabulary and comprehension activities being studied
- Conducting simulated tours around the classroom, the school, and the school community, using the content being studied
- Presenting fashion shows, festivals, and pageants to culminate the completion of units on clothing, food, holiday celebrations, etc.
- Creating a marketplace in the classroom, with different types of stores and services. Students move around, purchasing some things with fake money, bargaining in some cases, and learning about the differences between shopping at home and abroad.
- Creating motions by eliciting ideas from the children as they learn a new dialogue, poem, song, etc.
- Simulating travel in space, with conversations to ground control
- Developing "motion mnemonics, using a recorded rhythm instrument, for learning vocabulary
- Creating a "home" in the classroom in order to role-play family life in the foreign country and in the United States
- Planning a program for presentation to the rest of the school, on such themes as
    1. Songs and dances of the foreign culture
    2. Dramatization of foreign culture folk tales
    3. Dramatization of travel in the foreign country
    4. Dramatization of a scene at the United Nations
    5. Programs for special holidays
    6. Dramatization of the life of famous persons from the foreign culture
    7. Quiz program about people and places in the foreign culture
    8. Dramatization of well-known current events as seen by people in the foreign culture
    9. "Who Am I?" programs—interviews with person from the foreign culture

10. Interviews with foreign language speakers—contrasts with different aspects of culture

● Creating and using jazz chants that can be amusing, rhythmic (as the children clap hands or snap their fingers), and repetitious. Example:

La escuela, la escuela,
No me gusta, no me gusta;
Prefiero la playa
Me gusta la playa
No me gusta la escuela . . .

Many other types of TPR activities are possible at the elementary school level, and teachers should be ready to create (themselves or with the children) additional activities that will add a kinesthetic component that will promote maximum learning and vitalize the lessons.

For additional suggestions on TPR, see the Bibliography: Asher, 11; Krashen, 94; Larew, 103; Schneider, 179; and Segal, 183.

DRAMATIZING AND ROLE-PLAYING

Children of all ages enjoy role-playing and dramatizing activities. They enjoy dramatizing folk tales, and they get pleasure from activities that put them into the "shoes" of children in foreign cultures. All kinds of communicative activities, dialogues, stories, anecdotes, commercials, daily family life activities, and the like can be converted into some kind of dramatic form. The rehearsals are wonderful ways to have numerous repetitions and drills, since the ultimate goal is a fine performance. Through play, repetition, and practice, youngsters can absorb tremendous quantities of foreign language communicative expressions.

Even some of the nuances of language can be emphasized through drama techniques. Changing intonation patterns of the same sentence can help youngsters understand different patterns of meaning. Learning how to change one's voice so that it sounds like a five-year-old and later like a ninety-year-old can also convey much meaning, without, of course, including stereotypical behaviors. Some simple role-playing strategies can be

- Asking permission to do something at home; then at school
- Creating a scene with a complete conversation
- Creating a scene with just a few words of the conversation
- Creating a scene that expresses different emotions, such as happiness, sadness, boredom, illness, etc.
- Playing charades in the foreign language
- Impromptu situations based on random picking of cards from a box that may contain some of the following instructions:

> You are about to explain why you do not have your homework (possible explanation includes the fact that the dog ate it, you lost it, etc.)

> You and your friend picked up a $10.00 bill. You and your friend are discussing what should be done with it.

For additional suggestions on using role-playing and drama techniques in the classroom, see the Bibliography: MacRae, 130; Maley and Duff, 131; Moskowitz, 146; Omaggio, 155, 156; Sadow, 174; Savignon, 176; Smith, 187; Stanislawczyk and Yavner, 192.

HELPING CHILDREN LEARN

Children learn in different ways. Teachers too seldom know how children learn, and do not have the time to offer instruction in different modalities. Certainly, using the Total Physical Response approach helps to reinforce the learning, and teachers would be wise to use this approach when the content and the situation call for this helpful and enjoyable form of learning.

Other strategies are helpful, too. Many teachers find that in presenting new work of any kind (language, science, mathematics, etc.) it is helpful, if memory is involved, to point out or to elicit from the children ways in which they can remember. Mnemonics have proved to be helpful. Most Spanish language teachers remember the "shoe verbs" that highlight the stem changes. Teachers have encouraged children to remember the stem-changing verb forms, but also have encouraged creativity on the part of the children by having them design different types of shoes: ballet slippers, hockey shoes, etc.

(for stem-changing verbs in Spanish)

Graphic pictures of vocabulary words are fun and also reinforce the memory process. Words in Spanish, such as

GATO (cat)   and   ARBOL (tree)

pictorialized can enhance the learning. Very often, using an acronym (first letter of each word forms a new word) is a good example of something that helps students learn. Even if the new word is invented, it can be helpful, such as BRAVA for some of the major colors in Spanish: *blanco, rojo, amarillo, verde, azul.*

Any other kind of word-picture or word-word association cues can readily be created by both teachers and children. Class sessions devoted to the ways different children remember different things can be of lifelong benefit. Additional references for memory training can be found in the Bibliography: Birckbichler, 24; Collet, 35; Hunter, 85; Stevick, 200; Tuttle, 206.

ERROR CORRECTION

It is extremely helpful if students understand that they will make some errors while speaking, reading, and writing, and that they may not always understand what is being said, particularly in FLES and FLEX and early stages of immersion. In immersion, the language content and the subject-area content add to the student's anxiety about making mistakes, but as the student moves ahead in the grade levels, there is less and less concern about the foreign language content because of the excellent proficiency the students have developed.

Students ought to be made aware of different levels of proficiency; the times when 100 percent accuracy is required, and when casual communication will permit some errors. This is a departure from the past, when there was only one correct answer to the exercise in the text. Teachers may wish to elicit different answers and help the children to see that one answer might be appropriate between friends, while another answer would be most suitable while communicating with an adult.

This is the teacher's responsibility—not to be the person who constantly red-pencils every attempt at written work, not to correct every word uttered, but someone who defines clearly that ideas and concepts count and that communication must be suited to the situation, the people involved, and the level of expectation. This does not take away from the goal that students will be expected to learn how to use the foreign language correctly (in all four skills) and that for the most part, correct language is required in all test situations. But it is these nuances of language use that students need to learn, by explanation, by role-modeling, by suggestion, and by correction. Correction should be done in such a way that it will not suppress ideas and thinking skills. Where many students make similar errors, teachers will need to reteach specific elements or plan to teach concepts that may not have been reached, as yet.

TEACHING TECHNIQUES FOR "GIFTED" LANGUAGE LEARNERS

Most teachers with many years of experience can easily identify the "gifted" language learners—those students who learn easily and who experience few difficulties in learning the four basic skills of listening comprehension, speaking, reading, and writing in the language.

It is suggested here that teachers plan special ways to enrich these children's language abilities by having students

- serve as leaders of different kinds of class activities and games
- work on independent projects of interest to them (e.g., poetry, computer programs)
- use the foreign language in different types of impromptu situations
- listen to records or cassette tapes slightly above their level
- make presentations before the class or other classes (choral, dramatic, etc.)
- prepare special reports, riddles, etc., to be used with the rest of the class
- create language games for the rest of the class
- construct test items
- give spot dictations
- do research about the people who speak the foreign language
- give model responses for the rest of the class or ask questions of other students

Even on the elementary school level, differences in ability will be noted, and teachers should look for ways to stimulate these "gifted" language learners. Although some research has been conducted in this field, there is no concrete evidence that only gifted students (in general) should study a foreign language. It is recommended that all students be offered the opportunity to study a foreign language. However, there will always be some students who can listen carefully, who can pronounce the foreign language with accuracy and with very little effort, who seem to know how to get the gist of meaning from an utterance, and who do not experience great difficulty in writing the content of the language with accuracy. These are the students who require special attention and special encouragement, lest they become restless, bored, and worst of all, "turned off" of foreign language learning.

This was one of the problems of **FLES** in the sixties, when the emphasis was on long sequences, rote learning, pattern practice, and memorization of dialogues with rare opportunities for real-life situations and communication. This is not to say that repetition should be eliminated. Repetition is a necessary part of effective language learning, but youngsters need to achieve some end result of communication and need to feel the power of language through communicative experiences.

Children who have special talents in languages need special activities that will keep them interested and excited about using the language. In this respect, students in immersion programs acquire this sense of power, but because they are involved in a long sequence, even in immersion some of them may reach the preadolescent years and feel that they want to try something new. Unfortunately, in any long sequence, able and gifted students begin to think that the foreign language is "old hat." That is why it is essential for teachers to be sensitive to these students and to plan effective ways of keeping them interested. Appealing to higher-order thinking skills, by asking them to mention in the foreign language, similarities and differences between, for example, a hammer and a guitar, will perk up their powers of observation as well as their interest in the foreign language.

Using a brainstorming technique, in which there are no correct nor incorrect answers, can also provide challenges for children. Asking them for different uses for a paper clip, for example, or different uses for a half cup of soda can provide additional stimulation for all children. Depending on the goals of the program, this can be done in the foreign language, within the limits of what the children have been taught. This can easily be done in immersion programs and in grades 5 and 6 of a FLES program that began several years earlier.

For additional suggestions on creative activities that develop higher-order thinking skills, see the Bibliography: Sternberg, 197; Wasserman, 215.

TECHNIQUES FOR TEACHING LESS MOTIVATED YOUNGSTERS

With the wide range of abilities of youngsters in FLES, FLEX, and immersion classes, teachers need to consider special procedures for helping the less motivated students to learn. Whatever the reasons for diminished motivation may be, teachers need to address such factors as inattention, restlessness, boredom, confusion, lack of understanding, frustration, and others. Following are some suggestions for helping to ameliorate difficult situations:

- Motivate each activity so that children will want to participate
- Make certain that instructions are clear, understandable, and easy to follow
- Teach by way of the "small increment approach," using familiar materials and adding on a small amount of new material
- Review frequently, but use an interesting and different format
- Alternate listening-speaking activities with reading or writing activities
- Plan for 5 to 7 different activities during one class session of approximately 30 minutes. If shorter or longer, make the necessary adjustments.
- Use a game format frequently, for reinforcement of language learning
- Use abundant praise and encouragement
- Keep the pace of the lesson rapid, but not too rushed
- Stress routines and study skills as well as hints for remembering
- Try to get a response (at least one) from each and every student during each class session (but never force a response)
- Make certain that from time to time there is something "unexpected" planned
- Try to incorporate interesting and famous names, such as singers, TV personalities, sports heroes, etc.
- Try to guarantee some degree of success for each student
- Make sure that the students understand. Students lose interest if they cannot understand what is being said and what is being asked of them. This means that English has to be used for very short periods of time.
- Try to check youngsters' written work, as most students do not copy accurately. Check *all* written work. Use student helpers to assist.
- Be sure that students understand exactly what is expected of them. Not every word of vocabulary nor every expression needs to be learned for active use (speaking and writing).

- Pay special attention to difficult words. Use cross-language contrasts, repetition, discussion of the configuration of the word, individual memory triggers, etc.
- Make certain that the content is appropriate for the students' level of instruction. It should provide some challenge, but have sufficient familiar work so that frustration does not set in.
- When a number of children are restless (depending on the time of day, such as before or after lunch, right before dismissal time, etc.) it is time for a change-of-pace activity. Usually, a TPR activity will relieve the problem.
- Plan to use simple questions with the less motivated students so that they will have the experience of success.

SIMILARITIES BETWEEN FLES* METHODOLOGY AND SECONDARY SCHOOL METHODOLOGY

Use of English

Both methodologies tend to keep English to a minimum, with most instructions, directions, and explanations given in the target language, except at the very beginning. Use of real objects, gestures, pictures, and other visuals help to convey meaning. When there is confusion, it might be better to give a brief explanation in English. In immersion, however, all content and explanations are given in the target language with the exception of certain subjects such as music, physical education, and art, in some partial immersion programs.

Functional Language

With the new emphasis on proficiency, the two methodologies are closer in goals and content. Both now are concerned with functional situations and authentic utterances. Both do not always insist upon complete sentences, but mirror natural speech patterns. Both have a conversational approach in situations likely to occur. Vocabulary is taught in context, and all kinds of idiomatic phrases are included.

Use of the Textbook

Although more emphasis is placed on the textbook or textbooks in secondary schools, both levels tend to use a variety of text materials, such as a basic text, periodicals, readers, workbooks, and others. Teachers at both levels need to know how to adapt their text materials to their requirements, giving students ample opportunities to use all four skills and to gain an understanding of the cultural elements as well as the linguistic components.

Development of the Four Skills (Listening, Speaking, Reading, and Writing)

In both methodologies, the goals include the development of the four skills. Depending upon the goals of the type of **FLES** program, the amount of reading and writing skills may be considerably less than those in the secondary school program. This area is a point of departure for the two methodologies, although in sequential FLES programs and immersion, there are considerable amounts of reading and writing activities as an integral part of the program.

HIGHLIGHTS

- **There is no *one* way to teach FLES***

- **Methodology is determined by the goals, the participants, and the teacher**

- **The primary skills are listening, speaking, reading, writing, and culture for the purpose of communication**

VIII

Evaluation

GENERAL CONSIDERATIONS

In developing an evaluation design for FLES/FLEX/immersion programs, a number of factors should be included, such as:

- Performance of students in listening, speaking, reading, writing, and cultural awareness in the *foreign language* (For immersion students, in addition to the above, progress in all aspects of the elementary school curriculum, including successful results on standardized tests in mathematics and language, *in English*)
- Attitudes of students toward foreign language study
- Reactions of parents
- Reactions of principals and administrators
- Reactions of classroom teachers (if they do not teach the FL)
- Reactions of classroom teachers (if they are also the FL teachers)
- Reactions of foreign language teachers
- Reactions of volunteers who provide instruction
- Other reactions
- Overall evaluation of the program

The central idea in planning any evaluation is the matching of the goals and objectives to the evaluation procedures. It is an un-

132

sound procedure to implement a program in the elementary schools, and then when it is time to evaluate the program, to administer a standardized secondary school foreign language examination (which may have no relationship with the local objectives) just because no other test exists! Educators would never dream of handling evaluation of other subject areas in this way. The problem derives from the fact that there are no valid standardized foreign language tests for the elementary school level. Even if one could locate such an examination, there would not be a certainty that it measured what had been taught, since, elementary school FL program will differ greatly from district to district, from school to school, etc.

For these reasons, as was indicated in Chapter 4, it is of great importance that during the planning and organizing stage a design for evaluation be developed that will be in consonance with the local objectives and goals.

Another crucial question, to be determined at the local level, is who will conduct the evaluation. Will it be one or more persons within the school district? Will it be an outside consultant or a team of consultants? Will it be a combination of both inside and outside people? Will it be someone who understands a foreign language program, or will it be a research specialist? This author would urge that at least one person on a team be a foreign language specialist, so that there would be input when there are deliberations on the analysis of data and interpretations to be derived from the data.

Finally, as with any educational undertaking, the goals and objectives of the evaluation procedures must be determined in advance, with an indication of the kinds of evaluation instruments that will be used, and the kinds of evaluation instruments that will have to be developed. All of these functions, of course, should have been included in the planning budget for the program.

For aptitude tests, the reader is referred to the Bibliography: *French Achievement Test*, 63; Hancock *et al.*, 77; and Lipton, 119.

Currently, research people are developing new types of **FLES** evaluative instruments. C.L.E.A.R. (Center for Language Education and Research) is developing and field-testing a Spanish Achievement Test of Listening Comprehension, Reading, and Writing. The Center for Applied Linguistics is developing an adaptation of a classroom observation checklist originally developed by the Ontario Institute for Studies in Education (Toronto).

For additional information on testing foreign languages and evaluation procedures, see the Bibliography: Alexander and John, 2; Bartz, 21; Dammer *et al.*, 38; Dufort, 49; Joiner, 89; Lopato, 126; Oller, 152; Omaggio, 154; and Valette, 208.

For research studies evaluating the effectiveness of different types of **FLES** programs, see the Bibliography: Brega and Newell, 27; Campbell *et al.*, 30; Dunkel and Pillet, 51; Gray *et al.*, 74; Lambert and Tucker, 99; Landry, 100, 101; Lipton, 119, 120; Lopato, 126; Masciantonio, 135; Oneto, 157; Rafferty, 166; Rhodes and Snow, 167; Somerville, 188; and Vocolo, 212.

Overviews of research studies in the Bibliography are to be found in Donoghue, 45; Krashen *et al.*, 96; and Papalia, 160.

GUIDELINES FOR OVERALL ASSESSMENT OF THE FOREIGN LANGUAGE PROGRAM

Goals

1. What are the goals of the program?
2. Is there an advisory/steering committee?
3. Have parents and students been informed of the goals?
4. Does the instructional program reflect the goals?
5. Does the evaluation design reflect the goals?
6. How does the program fit in with the entire foreign language sequence? with the elementary school program?
7. Is it a pilot program, or is it an approved program?

Administration of the Program

1. Does instruction occur during the school day? When? How often ? Weekly time allotment?

2. What type of teacher provides the instruction?

3. What kind of certification does each teacher have? Has the teacher had a FLES/FLEX/immersion methods course and student teaching?

4. Is there a coordinator or supervisor of the program?

5. Does the teacher (or teachers) meet with secondary school teachers? How often? For what purpose?

6. Which materials are used for the program? How do they relate to the materials used in secondary school?

7. What is the language proficiency of the teacher(s)?

8. In what grade does the program begin?

9. How are the students selected (if at all)?

10. What is the time allotment and schedule (how many minutes per class, per grade; how many time a week)?

11. Which languages are taught? Which languages are taught in the secondary schools? What was the basis for the choice?

12. What is the plan for articulation of students moving from the elementary school to the middle/junior H.S.?

13. What provision is there for changing or modifying the program?

14. What is the dropout rate?

15. Is an eclectic approach used?

Instructional Program Checklist

1. Are all four skills presented, in a way consistent with the age, grade level, and abilities of the students?

2. Are cultural components included in class sessions?

3. Is there variety of presentation?

4. Is there participation of all students?

5. Is there variety of materials? Are authentic materials used?

6. How are youngsters corrected when they make errors?

7. Is each lesson carefully planned?

8. Is the foreign language used 90 to 99 percent of the time?

9. Do students get opportunities to use the language with partners or in small groups? Are other effective techniques used?

10. Do the children seem to be interested in the lessons?

11. Do the children speak the foreign language with some fluency and accuracy?

12. At the conclusion of a lesson, do the children know that they have learned something?

13. At the conclusion of the lesson, do the children indicate that they want to come back to the next lesson?

14. During the lessons, do students appear to understand the FL?

15. Does the teacher include Total Physical Response or movement?

16. Are the students able to read and write the foreign language?

17. Do the students know the places in the world where the foreign language is spoken?

18. Are resource people from the community and from the consulates invited to class?

19. Are students from the secondary schools invited to class? Are native speakers from the secondary schools invited to class?

20. Are elementary school students invited to participate in districtwide festivals, career activities, and other international events?

21. Is there a curriculum or course of study for each year of the program? What is the overall philosophy of the program?

22. Is a variety of media used in the program, including audio, visual, and computer?

23. Are students free from signs of boredom, fatigue, lack of participation? Do the students appear to be challenged and able to perform the required tasks?

24. Does the teacher assist individual students, both for remediation and enrichment?

25. Are the lessons well paced and interesting?

26. Do students understand why they are studying a foreign language?

Evaluation

1. Is there ongoing evaluation in the classroom?
2. Is there an evaluation design for the program?
3. Are students evaluated in listening comprehension, speaking, reading, writing, and cultural awareness according to the goals of the program? What kind of instrument is used for evaluation?
4. Are students graded for their foreign language work?
5. Is the program evaluated each year?
6. Are changes made on the basis of the evaluation?
7. Is an outside consultant invited to assist in evaluation?
8. Are there long-range plans for the program?
9. Does the community understand the goals of the program?
10. Do parents and students understand the goals of the program?
11. Does the advisory/steering committee contribute to the evaluation of the program?

Special Note about the Evaluation of Immersion Programs

There has been extensive evaluation of immersion programs in Canada. There are references in the Bibliography under Dulay *et al.*, 50; Krashen *et al.*, 96; Lambert and Tucker, 99; and Swain, 203.

For references on the evaluation of immersion programs in the United States, see the Bibliography: Campbell *et al.*, 30; Cohen, 34; Forsythe, 62; Genesee, 68; Howe, 83; Jacobs, 86; Ozete, 158; and Rhodes and Snow, 167.

GUIDELINES FOR OBTAINING REACTIONS OF PARENTS, PRINCIPALS AND ADMINISTRATORS, CLASSROOM TEACHERS, FOREIGN LANGUAGE TEACHERS, AND VOLUNTEERS

Probably the two most effective ways to obtain reactions from the above-mentioned persons would be questionnaire and person-to-person interviews. These should be geared to local goals.

Some of the questions that might be asked are

1. What is your opinion, in general, of the program?
2. Do you think the children have made progress in their use of the foreign language?
3. Do you think they enjoy learning a foreign language?
4. Have you heard references to the foreign language outside of the foreign language class?
5. Are the children interested in continuing their study of a foreign language?
6. How would you rate the effectiveness of the teacher of the foreign language(s)?
7. Is sufficient time in the school day being devoted to the study of a foreign language? Too much?
8. What is your opinion of the materials used in the foreign language program?
9. Does there seem to be a relationship between the study of a foreign language and other subjects in the elementary school curriculum?
10. What is the basis for your information about the foreign language program? (observation, discussion with child and/or children, etc.)
11. What changes would you recommend for the foreign language program?
12. Is there a smooth transition from this program to the middle/junior H.S.?

The following is a sample questionnaire for obtaining reactions of principals:

Questionnaire for Principals of Elementary Schools Having Foreign Language (Response 1 to 5)*

1. Most of the children understand the foreign language. __

2. Most of the children speak the foreign language. __

3. Most of the children enjoy learning a language. __

4. The instructor enjoys teaching a foreign language.
   __ Parent volunteer
   __ High school student
   __ Elementary school teacher

5. The classroom teacher is interested in the foreign language lesson. __

6. The classroom has foreign language displays. __

7. The time devoted to the foreign language has educational value. __

8. Most of the parents enjoy the language program. __

This could be adapted for parents, classroom teachers, students, etc.

For a more detailed questionnaire and results from questioning principals, see the Bibliography: Baranick and Markham, 17.

GUIDELINES FOR OBTAINING ATTITUDES OF STUDENTS

Attitudes of students studying a foreign language can be obtained by questionnaires, person-to-person interviews, and

*5 is the highest

observation of classes. The methods chosen depend on the age and grade levels of the students.

Some of the questions that might be asked are

1. Do you enjoy learning a foreign language?
2. Would you like to continue to study the foreign language next year?
3. Would you like to read stories in the foreign language?
4. Would you like to have a pen pal from the foreign culture?
5. Do you think you will remember what you learned?
6. Do you use the foreign language outside of the language class?
7. Do you come across articles and pictures about the foreign culture in newspapers and magazines?
8. Do you like the materials used in the foreign language class?
9. Is the foreign language connected to anything else you study at school?
10. Would you like to visit the foreign culture someday?
11. Is there enough time devoted to the foreign language class?
12. What changes would you recommend for the foreign language program?
13. Do you want to continue your study of the foreign language in middle/junior H.S.?
14. What do you like best about your foreign language teacher?
15. Do you understand why you are studying a foreign language?

GUIDELINES FOR OBTAINING REACTIONS OF CLASSROOM TEACHERS

There are probably three important ways to obtain reactions from teachers of FLES/FLEX/immersion. The use of a questionnaire is helpful; a person-to-person interview is even better. Observation of the teacher in the foreign language class is still another way to get the teacher's point of view.

Some of the questions that might be asked are

1. What is your opinion, in general, of the program?
2. Do you think the children have made progress in their use of the foreign language?
3. Do you think they enjoy learning a foreign language?
4. Do you enjoy teaching a foreign language to children?
5. Are the children interested in continuing their study of a foreign language?
6. Have the children complained about any aspect of their study of a foreign language?
7. Do the children bring in articles, objects, and pictures related to the foreign culture on their own?
8. Is sufficient time in the school day being devoted to the study of a foreign language? Too much?
9. What is your opinion of the materials used in the foreign language program?
10. Is there a relationship between the study of a foreign language and other subjects in the elementary school curriculum?
11. What happens to these children when they reach the middle/junior H.S.?
12. What changes would you recommend for the foreign language program?

A SELF-EVALUATION CHECKLIST FOR THE FLES* TEACHER

How do you know when you've taught an effective foreign language lesson? Ask yourself the following questions:

1. Are all students actively participating in the foreign language, either individually, in small groups, or in whole-class activities?
2. Are the youngsters given the opportunity to use the foreign language in functional situations during the lesson?
3. Are students able to use the language (depending on the goals

of the program) in all four skills of listening, speaking, reading, and writing? for higher-order thinking skills activities?

4. Have I planned a variety of activities in short segments?

5. Do I plan review and reinforcement activities as well as having a presentation of new work in each lesson?

6. Do I use a wide variety of auditory and visual materials of interest to young children? Do I sometimes plan a surprise?

7. Do I try to motivate each lesson and each part of the lesson?

8. Is there ongoing evaluation for purposes of diagnosis of problems as well as for grouping?

9. Are cultural topics woven into each foreign language lesson?

10. Is the textbook adapted and modified to suit the curriculum and the ability of the students?

11. Do I have effective classroom routines, so that everyone is on task during the entire lesson? Is every minute used?

12. Do I explain the new homework clearly? Do I check the homework (if any) each class session?

13. Do the students and I use the foreign language? Do I only very briefly explain something in English?

14. Do my students appear to look forward to the next FL lesson?

15. Do I look forward to the next FL lesson?

GUIDELINES FOR THE ASSESSMENT OF THE PERFORMANCE OF STUDENTS

Listening Comprehension: Does the Youngster Understand?

In order to test students' listening comprehension skills, a number of suggestions are listed below for assisting in the creation of tests at the local level (based on local goals):

- Teachers may use TPR commands to see if students understand and perform the action(s)
- Teachers may use double or even triple TPR commands

- Students see two or more objects drawn on a sheet of paper. In the sample below, the teacher will say aloud "the flag." Students will circle the picture that matches the utterance.

Sometimes, teachers may wish to prerecord (rather than say it aloud) and play the tape during class. Instead of using a paper with drawings on it, the teacher may say the utterance and the children will draw the object. (The students with artistic talents will only do well on this test if they understand what has been said in the FL.)

- An alternative to this type of test would be for the teacher to show flashcards, and students would have on their answer sheets **1. A B C D.** They would circle the letter of the picture that was shown as the teacher said the name of the object to be matched in the foreign language. For example, the teacher says "the chair" and then holds up each picture in turn:

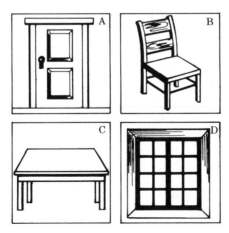

- Another variation would be that students would have a picture on their papers and the teacher would make a true-false statement about the picture. For example, for the picture below, the teacher says "There are three fish swimming in the lake." Students write "yes" or "no" on their papers.

For upper grades (5 and 6), the students could be required to correct the statement when they have written "no." This would then make it a combined listening comprehension and writing test item.

- A more advanced listening comprehension test item would be listening to a short paragraph, then a question, then repetition of the short paragraph and the question. Students would have three or four answers on their answer sheet; they would read all the possible answers and circle the one that seems to be the best answer.

  Teacher reads:

  Mary is sick. She has a headache. She is going to her aunt's house with her father. Her aunt is a doctor. Her uncle is not home.

  Question: Who is a doctor?

  The student reads on the answer sheet and circles one answer:

  a. Mary's father is a doctor.
  b. Mary is a doctor.
  c. Mary's uncle is a doctor.
  d. Mary's aunt is a doctor.

This, too, is not purely listening comprehension, as it combines listening comprehension and reading.

Speaking Proficiency: Is the Youngster Communicating?

In order to test students' speaking proficiency skills, a number of suggestions are listed below for assisting in the creation of tests at the local level (based on local goals):

- Answering direct questions, such as "How are you?"
- Asking students to ask someone something, such as "Ask Jack how old he is."
- Asking students to describe what they see in a picture
- Asking two students to "perform" an impromptu situation
- Showing students two types of food and asking them which one they would choose
- Asking students to take the part of the teacher for a class activity
- For more advanced students, showing students a series of three pictures and asking them to tell a story about them:

- Another activity would be to ask one student to perform a TPR activity and ask a second student to describe in the foreign language what the first student was doing

The question of how to rate items on a speaking test sometimes is a problem. First, a decision must be made about which aspects of the responses are to be rated. For example, such items as appropriateness of response, pronunciation, fluency, accuracy, and comprehensibility of the response may each receive 1 point for a maximum of 5 on a global rating scale. Local areas may wish to list their own criteria for grading speaking proficiency. See "Error Correction" in Chapter 7.

Reading Comprehension: Does the Youngster Get Meaning from the Printed Page?

In order to test students' reading comprehension skills, a number of suggestions are listed below for assisting in the creation of tests at the local level (based on local goals):

- Match pictures with words
- Match words with descriptions of the words
- Make columns of related words from a list of words
- Completion of sentences from a choice of three or four. *For example:*

    The weather is bad. _____
    - a. The sun is shining.
    - b. It is raining.
    - c. The sky is blue.

- Read a short paragraph. Selecting an answer to a question from a choice of three or four. *For example:*

    Bob has three pets. He has a black cat, a green parrot, and a goldfish. The parrot is singing. The cat is playing with a ball. The goldfish, Carl, is swimming.

    Question: What is the cat doing?
    - a. It is singing.
    - b. It is swimming.
    - c. It is playing.
    - d. Its name is Carl.

- Solve a riddle from a choice of possibilities. *For example:*

    It is big. It is green and brown. It is not an animal. What is it?
    - a. A house
    - b. A tree
    - c. A chair
    - d. A door

Writing Skills: Is the Youngster Communicating in Writing?

In order to test students' writing skills, a number of suggestions are listed below for assisting in the creation of tests at the local level (based on local goals):

- Writing captions for pictures
- Taking a short dictation
- Writing answers to oral questions
- Writing answers or rejoinders to written questions or statements
- Rewriting a sentence (e.g., in the negative form) or beginning the sentence with "On July 4, _____."
- Rewriting a false statement (e.g., "Today it is snowing.")
- Writing a letter to a friend (guided composition) telling him or her about your school, your teacher, etc.
- Writing a letter to a friend (not guided)
- Writing a poem
- Writing a short composition based on a picture, a folk song, sounds in the street, etc.
- Writing an invitation to a party
- Completing sentences (e.g., Because the weather is bad we will not go fishing. We will _____.)

The rating of writing is quite similar to the rating of speaking. A decision must be made about which aspects of the responses are to be rated. For example, such items as appropriateness of response, fluency, accuracy, and comprehensibility may each receive 1 point for a maximum of 4 on a global rating scale. Local areas may wish to list their own criteria for grading writing skills. Many school systems are using a global or holistic approach to grading written skills in English. This can easily be adapted to grading written work in the foreign language.

Cultural Awareness: Does the Youngster Understand Differences and Similarities Between the Cultures?

Evaluation of cultural awareness will depend on the concepts and cross-cultural topics in the curriculum at the local level.

Here are a few examples of the types of evaluative questions that could be developed in this area:

- Subjective response completions, graded only on the appropriateness of response. *For example:*
  When I see a picture of the Eiffel Tower, I think _____.

- Questionnaires based on the content of the classwork and discussions, with such items as: *True or false, and give your reasons: All Spaniards are happy.*

- TPR role-plays by groups of children. *For example:*   .
  One group of children role-playing watching a bullfight in Spain. Another group of children role-playing watching a baseball game in the United States. Class discussion about similarities and differences from the observers' point of view; from the participants' point of view.

- Role-plays of the celebration of holidays. *For example:*
  a national holiday in the United States and a national holiday in Germany

- Class responds to cultural assimilators (see the section on cultural awareness in Chapter 6) and discusses why each response has merit, or why it may be incorrect. As a challenge to gifted students, they may be asked to create their own cultural assimilators after doing research about the foreign culture.

- Class discussion about the meaning of colors in the United States and in the target culture (e.g., Is pink always an indication of happiness?)

- Interviews with guest speakers who are native to the target culture, involving preparation of questions before the interview and followup activities after the interview

- Compositions depicting a contrast between the life of a school child in the United States and the life of a school child in the target culture

There are no standardized tests on measuring cultural awareness. What are not needed are tests of identification of cities, rivers, mountains, etc. What is needed is quite difficult to do—that is, an exploration of customs, daily life, holidays, and many cross-cultural comparisons, discussions, observations, thoughts, and feelings.

HIGHLIGHTS

- Does the youngster understand the foreign language?

- Is the youngster communicating in the foreign language?

- Does the youngster get meaning from the printed page?

- Is the youngster communicating in writing?

- Does the youngster understand differences and similarities between the cultures?

IX

Selection of Materials

The key word in the selection of materials for FLES, FLEX, and immersion is *variety*. Young children, overstimulated by the rapid images of early television viewing, are easily bored by the use of the same kinds of materials, such as pictures and flashcards. On the other hand, children adore the use of a puppet or puppets with whom they can identify and emphathize, and whom they can hug or chastise, according to the situations created by the teacher. Thus, teachers are dealing with two basic needs: the need for "new" and "exciting," and the need for the "known" and the "secure."

With the constantly evolving technology in instructional materials, and with publishers developing completely integrated packages with different kinds of components, one would think that there are sufficient materials of instruction. We are going to approach a satisfactory pool of materials within the next few years, but school districts and teachers need to be aware of some of the criteria for selection of appropriate materials. They also need to be reminded that because every class of students is different, a number of supplementary materials will always be needed, particularly if the goals of the program include group work and individualization of instruction, to some extent.

CRITERIA

The following criteria represent some of the points to be considered when selecting materials of instruction:

1. Do the materials satisfy the goals of the program?

2. Do the materials carry out the objectives for the grade level?

3. Are the materials developed in such a way that they can be adapted easily for the specific needs of a specific class?

4. Do the materials include a wide range of activities appealing to different learning modalities and styles?

5. Do the materials include a number of components that fit together well for the delivery of the goals of the program?

6. Are the materials of interest to children? Will they motivate the students to learn? Are they appropriate for their age?

7. Are the materials attractive? Are the pictures important to the content? Do they have eye-appeal?

8. Do the materials contain effective cultural components? Do they avoid stereotypes?

9. Are the materials free from bias? Is a contrast made between standards in the United States and those in other countries?

10. Do the materials reflect sequential development? Are they articulated with middle school and secondary school materials?

11. Are concepts clearly delineated, illustrated, highlighted?

12. Are all four skills included in the plan of operation?

13. Is an evaluation plan included in the materials? Are there periodic checkpoints?

14. Do the materials include additional suggestions for the gifted student? the less able student? (particularly in the teachers' manual)

15. Do the materials include activities for TPR as well as cognitive activities?

16. Do the materials appeal to the senses and emotions of young children as well as to their curiosity?

17. Does humor appear from time to time in the materials?

18. Do the materials suggest enrichment with computer programs, video, and other types of the more recent technology?

19. Do the materials indicate the type of program for which they are suitable (e.g., FLES, FLEX, immersion, partial immersion)?

20. Are the materials "doable"? Is the content appropriate?

21. Are there suggestions for adapting the materials if the time schedule is severely curtailed? extended?

22. Are the strategies effective and worthwhile?

23. Is the pace satisfactory for the program and its goals?

24. Have the materials been field-tested? for what type of program? for what type of grade and class?

25. Is there is an audio component? Are the voices native or near-native, clear, well-paced?

26. Was the material planned for American students or foreign students? How important is this for the class(es)?

27. Are the materials easy to use? by an experienced teacher? by a beginning teacher? by a nonforeign language teacher? by a volunteer?

28. Do the materials seem to follow any particular language teaching philosophy? Does there seem to be an eclectic approach?

29. Do the materials fulfill the goals expressed by the author(s)?

30. Does an element of surprise appear in the materials from time to time?

31. Can the materials be used as a basic text, or are they to be considered supplementary?

32. Is there a teachers' manual? How helpful is it?

33. Is English included? How much? Too much?

34. Are there suggestions for followup and homework?

35. Are there explanations? Are they helpful?

36. Is there frequent review and re-entry?

37. Is there variety of format? language? topics?

38. Do the materials reflect a prereading stage? a prespeaking stage?

39. Which other components are available? Will they enhance the learning?

40. Is the cultural material integrated with the linguistic elements?

41. Can the materials be adapted for use in several grades?

WHAT KIND OF MATERIALS ARE USED IN FLES*?

posters	all kinds of toys	classroom objects
maps	food, clothing, and	and places in the
books	other real objects	school
magazines	greeting cards	places in the
pictures	travel brochures	neighborhood
flashcards	computer programs	photographs (very
flannelboard	transparencies	effective if taken
magnetboard	videocassettes	by students)
pocket charts	film	teacher-made and
records	television	student-made
audiocassettes	newspapers	materials

A Word about Teacher-Made Materials

Every effective teacher uses teacher-made materials to enrich, supplement, provide differentiated tasks for different types of learners, provide materials that supplement inadequate commercial materials, and relate to the specific goals and objectives of the local program. As teachers gain experience and familiarity with the needs and interests of their students, they become adept at creating stimulating and interesting support materials in FLES, FLEX, and immersion. For all the effort involved, however, teachers should exercise caution in the development of these "ditto sheets" by following these recommendations:

- Instructions should be clear.
- Copy should be legible, printed or typed.
- Worksheet should have eye-appeal and be of interest to children.
- Content should be appropriate to the goals and the level and ability of the children
- Materials should supplement, enrich, reinforce, and add variety to the program.
- Pictures and other visuals should accompany the written work.
- Content should be in correct, authentic foreign language.
- Complete sentences need not be expected of students at all

times. The dialogue or conversation should be appropriate to a real situation.

- Generally, worksheets should attempt to reinforce only *one* linguistic concept at early levels.

- Sentence structure should be parallel, and progress to more difficult patterns.

- Explanations should be brief, often accompanied by a clear diagram or visual.

- Every teacher-made sheet should have a specific purpose.

- Teachers should try to develop rapid means for both checking and student correction.

- Teachers should remember that students learn better through different modalities. Therefore, some attempt should be made to correlate with cassette recordings and visuals.

Materials for Immersion Programs

According to practitioners in the field, it is difficult to obtain appropriate materials for immersion programs. Generally, materials are used from foreign sources (French materials from Canada and France; Spanish materials from Spain, Mexico, and Latin America, etc.). Most of these materials, however, need to be adapted for immersion programs in U.S. schools, since they do not follow the guidelines for the U.S. elementary school curriculum.

For these reasons, materials for immersion programs need to be supplemented by district-created guidelines and other support materials for teachers, students, and parents.

Based on the Milwaukee experience, the following materials or curriculum products were deemed necessary for their French program (these could be adapted to any language):

- Annotated list of publishers of French materials suitable for grades K–6
- Expressions in English and French
- Menus in French

- French vocabulary and expressions (classroom objects, clothing, classroom expressions)
- Useful French expressions
- Expressions in French for kindergarten
- Helping parents learn a second language with their children
- Vocabulary for physical education
- French first grade reading units
- Penmanship—first grade
- Prereading unit
- Summer reading booklet—first grade
- Chart stories for first grade
- Short stories and activities
- Science unit on seeds
- Cursive writing unit—third grade
- How Do I Feel? and I Don't Feel Well
- French basic word list flashcards
- French vowel flashcards
- French phonics flashcards

These may be obtained at minimal cost from
     Curriculum Products
     Division of Curriculum and Instruction
     Milwaukee Public Schools, P.O. Drawer 10K
     Milwaukee, WI 53201-8210

Suggested Sources of Materials

Fortunately, there is a growing number of sources of effective materials for all types of FLES and FLEX programs. Currently, there are still too few immersion materials produced in the U.S., and too frequently foreign materials are not appropriate for students in the United States. This then necessitates much textbook adaptation and revision. Foreign materials sometimes include pictures and other types of supplementary materials that may be unacceptable to local school district standards for materials. It is hoped that more publishers will see fit to produce effective materials for immersion programs in the content areas of social studies, mathematics, science, language arts, and other areas.

The following represents a list of sources for materials for teachers and students, appropriate for FLES, FLEX, or immersion:

Professional Organizations

American Association of Teachers of French (AATF)
57 Armory Ave.
Champaign, IL 61820   (Publications, realia exhibits)

American Association of Teachers of German (AATG)
523 Bldg., Ste. 201
Rte. 38
Cherry Hill, NJ 08034   (AV aids Depository)

American Association of Teachers of Spanish and Portuguese (AATSP)
Mississippi State University
Mississippi State, MS 39762   (Culture units)

American Council on the Teaching of Foreign Languages (ACTFL)
P.O. Box 408
Hastings-on-Hudson, NY 10706   (Publications)

Brigham Young University
Center for International and Area Studies
Provo, UT 84602   (Publications)

Center for Applied Linguistics
1118 22 St., NW
Washington, DC 20037   (Publications)

C.L.E.A.R.
(Center for Language Education and Research)
1100 Glendon Ave.
Los Angeles, CA 90024   (Publications, tests)

Modern Language Association (M.L.A.)
10 Astor Place
New York, NY 10003   (Publications)

National FLES, FLEX, Immersion Commission of A.A.T.F.
University of Maryland/Baltimore County
Dept. Modern Languages/Linguistics (M.L.L.)
Catonsville, MD 21228　(Reports, materials center)

National Network for Early Language Learning
c/o C.A.L. (Center for Applied Linguistics)
1118 22 St., NW
Washington, DC 20037　(Newsletter)

New York State Association of Foreign Language* Teachers
(N.Y.S.A.F.L.T.)
1102 Ardsley Rd.
Schenectady, NY 12308　(Publications)

Northeast Conference on the Teaching of
　Foreign Languages**
Box 623
Middlebury, VT 05753　(Publications, media)

Ontario Institute for Studies in Education (O.I.S.E.)
252 Bloor St. W.
Toronto, Ontario M5S IVs Canada　(Publications)

Organization of American States
17th Street and Constitution Ave., NW
Washington, DC 20006　(Publications)

Suggested Sources of Materials for FLES, FLEX, and Immersion

This is a selected list of publishers, just to get you started. Send for catalogues, make inquiries, do further research, and you will discover many other sources of materials for your program.

Addison-Wesley Co.
Reading, MA 01867

---

*and other state foreign language organizations
**and other regional foreign language conferences

Adler's Foreign
Books/Midwest
European Publications
915 Foster
Evanston, IL 60201

Audio Forum
96 Broad St.
Guilford, CT 06437

Barron's Educational Series
250 Wireless Blvd.
Hauppauge, NY 11788

Berlitz Publications
866 Third Ave.
New York, NY 10022

Bilingual Educational
Services
2514 S. Grand Ave.
Los Angeles, CA 90007

Cambridge University Press
32 E. 57 St.
New York, NY 10022

Children's Press
1224 W. Van Buren St.
Chicago, IL 60607

Continental Book Co.
80-00 Cooper Ave.
Glendale, NY 11385

Editions Soleil
P.O. Box 847
Welland, Ontario L3B5Y5
Canada

Europa Bookstore
3229 N. Clark St.
Chicago, IL 60657

French and Spanish Book
Corp.
115 Fifth Ave
New York, NY 10003

Gessler Publishing Co.
900 Broadway
New York, NY 10003

Goldsmith's Music Shop
301 E. Shore Rd.
Great Neck, NY 11023

Harper and Row
(Newbury House Div.)
10 E. 53 St.
New York, NY 10022

Hatier-Didier
2805 M St., NW
Washington, DC 20007

D.C. Heath
125 Spring St.
Lexington, MA 02173

Iaconi
300 Pennsylvania Ave.
San Francisco, CA 94107

Ideal Foreign Books
132-10 Hillside Ave.
Richmond Hill, NY 11418

Iowa State University Press
Ames, Iowa 50010

Independent School Press
51 River St.
Wellesley Hills, MA 02181

The Kiosk
19223 De Havilland Dr.
Saratoga, CA 95020

Langenscheidt Publishers
46-35 54th Rd.
Maspeth, NY 11378

Larousse
572 Fifth Ave.
New York, NY 10036

Lectorum Publications
137 W. 14 St.
New York, NY 10011

Librairie Dussault
8955 Boulevard St. Laurent
Montreal, Canada

Lingo Fun
P.O. Box 986
Westerville, OH 42881

National Geographic Society
17th and M St., NW
Washington, DC 20036

National Textbook Co.
4255 W. Touhy
Lincolnwood, IL 60646

Polyglot Productions
P.O. Box 668
Cambridge, MA 02238-0668

Rand McNally
P.O. Box 7600
Chicago, IL 60680

Santillana Publishers
257 Union St.
Northvale, NJ 07647

Scholastic Inc.
730 Broadway
New York, NY 10003

Silver Burdette Co.
250 James St.
Morristown, NJ 07960

Sky Oakes Publishers
P.O. Box 1102
Los Gatos, CA 95031

SUMO Co.
1005 Debra Lane
Madison, WI 53704

Teacher's Discovery
1130 E. Big Beaver
Troy, MI 48083-1997

Wible Language Institute
24 S. 8th St.
Allentown, PA 18105

World Press
135 W. 29 St.
New York, NY 10001

Other sources

State departments of education in various states

Airlines

National airlines of the foreign country or countries

National railroads of the foreign country or countries

Cultural and commercial services of consulates of foreign countries

Foreign language bookstores

Department stores

Music and record stores

Public and university libraries

PR for FLES*—How to Get Publicity for Your Program

It pays to advertise. When you have a good product, it is important to let people know about it. Whether it is called PR, public relations, public awareness, or publicity, everyone concerned with the program needs to be involved in publicity, lest it die a slow death because of nonexistence in the eyes of the public.

Who is this public? The public consists of the people in the community, in the school: students, teachers, principals and administrators, guidance counselors, health personnel, food and janitorial staff, parents, taxpayers of all kinds, and more.

There are some people who think that you do not publicize until the program has been running successfully for several years. This author does not agree with that philosophy. If the program has been very carefully planned, with input from many, many people, then the publicity will invite additional input from, perhaps, untouched sources, and that can only be a positive affirmation for the program.

There are others who feel that "hype" for a program, to use the vernacular for developing public awareness, is not a professional activity, is unworthy of educational goals. This point of view is not valid in today's world of accountability and taxpayers' sense of economy. Obviously, programs that go unnoticed and unpublicized do not capture the attention of policymakers. The first and foremost premise is that the program *has* to be educationally sound and effective, in terms of what the students are accomplishing. But a sound and effective program need not go unnoticed and unpublicized. As a matter of fact, having students demonstrate their achievements in the foreign language will help the program. It will also communicate to the students that they are, indeed, making great strides in their study of the foreign language.

Effective PR can really help FLES/FLEX/immersion programs by giving opportunities to explain the program, publicize the goals and the activities, and demonstrate what the children have accomplished. PR sells everything we come in contact with, so why not use it to help sell a *good* program?

Who is your public? These are the people who need to know about your program:

Students in the school and
  feeder schools
Parents
Grandparents
Members of the community
Faculty of universities
Teachers of other disciplines
Taxpayer groups
Business organizations
Religious groups
Senior citizen groups
Educational associations
Veterans' groups

Scouts
Fraternal organizations
International organizations
Travel agencies
Administrators
Members of the school board
Guidance counselors
Other personnel in the
  schools
Local elected and appointed
  officials
Other

SUCCESSFUL PUBLIC AWARENESS

Here are some essential components of a successful public awareness program for FLES, FLEX, and immersion:

- Organize a committee (perhaps a subcommittee of the original steering committee. Be sure to include the principal!)
- Discuss these major questions:
    1. What is our objective?
    2. Who is our public? (our audience?)
    3. What is our product? What is the specific event?
- Plan a long-range program that will be continuous and on-going

The PR planning grid can be of assistance in planning a year-long sequential PR program.

PR PLANNING GRID

Steps	Date	Staff	Other Students	Parents	Guidance Counselors	County people	Other Educators	Press/ Media	Bd. of Ed. members	Others
1										
2										
3										
4										
5										
6										

1. What is being done?
2. How effective are we?
3. What would we like the response to be?
4. What can we do to improve and change the response?

- Divide your audience into two segments: in the school and the school community; beyond the school and the school community
- Designate someone as the contact person
- Establish personal contacts with the media
- Plan for publicity before, during, and after an event
- Be scrupulously accurate with names, dates, places, etc.
- Show appreciation when you get publicity
- Plan to take black-and-white glossy pictures that can be submitted after an event (be sure to get everyone's name). Show children in action!
- Write press releases tersely, one page if possible
- Try to get specific information on deadlines, and work around them
- Be sure to give credit where it is due
- Stick to the facts!
- Have everything and everyone ready when reporters and photographers come to the school
- Don't be disappointed if you're turned down. Perhaps reporters will be able to come next time.

Stories that may be of interest to the media include

- followup success story of a student who started foreign language at the elementary school and is now in J.H.S. or S.H.S.
- students who have done unusually well
- students who have used foreign language to perform a community service
- new and interesting methods of instruction
- a project being carried out in an unusual fashion
- a resource person from the community or from the embassy making a presentation to a class
- a success story of a teacher
- professional honors, awards, grants awarded to a teacher or supervisor of foreign languages

- unusual travel experience of a teacher or supervisor
- reactions of students to a new program
- international students visiting the area

GETTING PUBLICITY FOR SPECIAL EVENTS

One of the most important aspects of PR for **FLES** is to know how to reach the media, be it radio, TV, newspapers, or whatever.

Something as basic as writing a clear, legible, appealing press release is invaluable in helping to inform the public.

The basics of a press release are

- What is happening (specifically)?
- What is the background (brief)?
- When is it happening?
- Who is involved? Who is sponsoring it?
- Who is invited to come?
- What time?
- Is there a fee?
- Who is the contact person? Phone number?

Press releases should be sent to the education editor of local newspapers at least two weeks before an event at the school, with a schedule of the event. A followup telephone call should be made three to four days in advance, giving further details and discussing the best time of day for action photographs. After the event, be sure to thank the newspaper office for their assistance, whether you have received wide publicity or a three-line notice in the newspaper. Next time, maybe you will get better results!

GETTING PUBLICITY IN SCHOOL AND IN THE SCHOOL COMMUNITY

There are a number of ways in which FLES/FLEX/ immersion teachers and students can make the foreign language

Sample Press Release

Date _____

ANNOUNCING
A FOREIGN LANUAGE FESTIVAL

SATURDAY, MARCH 31, 19__

at the
BELTON WOODS ELEMENTARY SCHOOL

FOREIGN LANGUAGE FUN FOR CHILDREN AND
ADULTS!

11:00 A.M.–4:00 P.M.

THERE WILL BE MULTICULTURAL DISPLAYS,
MINILESSONS IN FOREIGN LANGUAGES, ETHNIC
FOOD BOOTHS, DISPLAYS OF STUDENT WORK AND
ACTIVITIES, SKITS, DANCES, GAMES.

YOU DO NOT HAVE TO KNOW A FOREIGN LANGUAGE
TO ATTEND AND ENJOY THE FESTIVITIES. THE
PUBLIC IS INVITED, AND ADMISSION IS FREE. FOR
FURTHER INFORMATION, CALL _____

Contact Person

Tel. No. _____

Best time to call: _____

---

program more visible. The very nature of the study of foreign languages (particularly in immersion) is to use the language all day. This connotes a certain exclusivity and aloofness from the rest of the school. If the public is to become aware of the achievements of students involved in the study of a foreign language (be it FLES, FLEX, or immersion), then a number of procedures might be tried in order to bring foreign language into the basic curriculum for the elementary school:

- As a homework assignment, have foreign language students teach non–foreign language students some basic greetings and phrases
- Have cultural displays on bulletin boards and showcases
- Prepare an assembly program on the language and culture, such as:

  —songs and dances
  —skits showing how students learn the foreign language
  —travel scenes in a foreign country
  —skits at airports and train terminals
  —humorous skits about lost baggage, lost passengers, etc.
  —programs for special holidays, such as Pan American Day or July 14 (Bastille Day) held during the school year
  —skits about famous people from the foreign culture, such as Louis Pasteur or Mozart or Columbus, etc.
  —challenges for the audience with riddles in the FL and/ or charades
  —skits showing famous historical and important events as seen by the people in the foreign country, such as the landing on the moon, or the election of a new president or the baseball world series
  —mini musicals or operas presented by the FL class
  —skits or puppet shows about fairy tales or children's stories
  —special program showing careers using foreign languages (children are interested even in elementary school)

- Designate a day to wear something from the foreign culture (hats, banners, iron-ons, etc.)
- Make an announcement bilingually over the loudspeaker (This would be a wonderful occasion for more advanced FL students to use their knowledge functionally)
- Hold a foreign language spelling bee
- Write letters to students in other language classes in the school (and to other classes in the school district)
- Have students contribute to a foreign language magazine or newspaper (also contribute articles to the school paper)

- Hold a poster contest in the school for FL and non-FL students
- Make birthday cards and seasonal cards with foreign language poems and captions
- Label different parts of the school building in the foreign language(s)
- On special occasions, have the school menu devoted to the foreign culture or cultures (with printed menus)
- Teach folk dances from the culture to all students
- Organize a mini-Olympics Day for the school with team names in the foreign language
- Show travel films of the foreign culture
- Describe a "mystery teacher" in the foreign language. Other students are to guess who it is
- Send letters and newsletters home frequently
- Ask for feedback through questionnaires and at meetings
- Have the principal develop a written proclamation (which could be read over the loudspeaker on the occasion of Foreign Language Day or National Foreign Language Week
- Have a bumper sticker contest about studying foreign languages, such as "Smile if You Speak a Foreign Language"
- Invite foreign language speakers to classes and to the school
- Write foreign language slogans on posters and bulletin boards (e.g., proverbs, mystery foreign language speaker, etc.)
- Have a display of books and magazines from the foreign culture in the classroom, the library, and the media center
- Have students design and wear buttons advertising brief expressions in the foreign language or about the foreign languages, such as:

> I FLIP FOR FLES
> FRENCH IS FANTASTIQUE
> SÍ FOR SPANISH
> GÜTEN TAG IS TERRIFIC

- Develop an immersion day for foreign language students (perhaps over a weekend) for a camping trip, for example, at an outdoor recreation facility or park
- Invite speakers from foreign embassies
- Have local business people visit the school to discuss job opportunities for students who speak a foreign language
- Show the country of origin (on a large map of the world) of the teachers and supervisors, perhaps going back several generations
- Invite the faculty from a local college or university to speak at an assembly
- Invite personnel from a local hospital or Red Cross unit to discuss their need to know a foreign language
- Plan a foreign language fair or festival for the school, parents, and the school community, with foods from various foreign cultures

Sample flyer for an International Fair

Special Hints on Organizing a FLES* Foreign Language Festival

1. Get support from teachers, administrators, parents, and members of the community.
2. Get 3 to 5 people to assume leadership roles.
3. Tie the festival in with schoolwide competitions, such as a poster contest, for example.
4. Make sure that you have chairpersons for the following key activities:
    Publicity
    Games
    Decorations
    Food
    Cleanup
    Entertainment
    Printing
    Buttons
    Bumper stickers
    Language-learning booths
    Other ideas appropriate at the local level
5. Two weeks before the festival, walk through the areas of the school with the key people.
6. Designate an area for coats.
7. Arrange for parking facilities.
8. Arrange for first aid, if necessary.
9. Designate an area for the festival headquarters.
10. The day before the festival, set up decorations.
11. Assign at least two people to be responsible for troubleshooting problems during the festival.
12. The day of the festival, ENJOY!
13. After the festival is over, clean up the school.
14. Thank everyone involved.
15. Hold a planning committee meeting to evaluate the success of the festival and to make plans and decisions about next year's festival.

This is an enormous undertaking, but it can run smoothly if each key person does the job with care and with enthusiasm. It is important that each of the key people is informed of all plans and decisions, so that people do not work at cross purposes. After a trial run at the school level, people on the planning committee may want to think in terms of a festival on a broader scale (districtwide and on all school levels). Special note: If a Foreign Language Festival is already in existence, FLES/FLEX/immersion teachers, students, and parents may want to volunteer their services so that they can be included.

Develop an attractive brochure about the program (FLES, FLEX, or immersion), giving information about the following:

Rationale for the program
Students who are eligible
Objectives of the program
Scheduling
Methodology
Results on standardized tests
Materials of instruction
Transportation (if needed)
Recognition outside the school district
Articulation
Quotes from students, parents, principals, etc.

Present awards to outstanding students and winners of various competitions (such as spelling bee, poster contest) like the sample below.

**BELTON WOODS ELEMENTARY SCHOOL
FOREIGN LANGUAGE AWARD**

Palma Nobilis   *Prix d'honneur*

Documento de Mérito   *Verdienst Bescheinigung*

_____

Name of student

Language _____   *Teacher* _____

Date _____   Principal _____

- Plan a balloon sendoff with postcards attached, written in the foreign language. Offer prizes for the return of the postcard from the farthest location.
- Prepare articles for the PTA newsletter.
- Get some air time at the local radio station with a public announcement something like the following:
  Visitors from many other lands come to this country. They bring with them their own language and culture, and they learn English. We need more Americans who can speak foreign languages, and we need to start children learning foreign languages early. Languages in the grades are inherently important for the children, for the school, for the state, and for our country. Let's start foreign languages early!
- Offer mini language lessons or songs for senior citizen groups and other community groups.
- Organize an art exhibit with an international theme.
- Plan a piñata-making demonstration or contest.
- Hold a contest to guess the number of beans in a jar by writing the number in the foreign language.

- Organize a class trip to a foreign restaurant. This requires careful planning ahead of time with the management.
- Develop a recipe booklet of recipes around the world. Parents and grandparents like to help in a project of this kind.
- Plan with other teachers in the school projects on interdisciplinary aspects of the foreign culture (e.g., explorers in social studies, posters in art, songs in music, etc.)
- Develop many other activities on the local level, appropriate to the school and the school community.
- Celebrate National Foreign Language Week with all kinds of activities.
- Organize an essay contest on "Why Study Foreign Languages?"

GETTING PUBLICITY BEYOND THE SCHOOL

Going beyond the school and the school community requires collaboration with foreign language teachers and others on secondary school levels. Activities planned for a wider audience require more elaborate planning and more enthusiastic people. Some of the activities for a districtwide public awareness program on all school levels might include the following:

- Planning a districtwide foreign language festival, including FLES/FLEX/immersion students
- Planning a districtwide camping experience, using the foreign language as much as possible. This type of experience can also be used as a motivational device. For example, at the University of Maryland/Baltimore County, an International Language Camp has been in operation for several years, with the goal of exposing 9- to 11-year-olds to a different language and culture each *day*. Words and phrases, customs, songs, dances, and guest speakers form the language content. This "Language a Day" concept can be incorporated into camps on the local level, along with the usual swimming, outdoor games, and dramatic activities.
- Placing posters and student project displays in local stores, libraries, museums, and other public places

● Having students teach the foreign language to shoppers at a shopping mall or at a large department store or at a county education fair. Some of the dialogues that could be taught briefly at such an activity could be adapted from the sample lessons given.

French

SPEAKER 1: Bonjour! Je m'appelle _____. (Hi! My name is _____.)

SPEAKER 2: Bonjour! Je m'appelle _____. (Hello! Mine is _____.)

SPEAKER 3: Vous parlez français très bien. (You speak French very well.)

SPEAKER 2: Merci. Vous êtes un bon professeur. (Thank you. You're a good teacher.)

SPEAKER 1: Merci, j'aime parler français. (Thanks, I like speaking French.)

SPEAKER 2: Au revoir. (Goodbye.)

SPEAKER 1: A bientôt. (See you later.)

German

SPEAKER 1: Tag! Ich heisse _____. (Hi! My name is _____.)

SPEAKER 2: Guten Tag! Ich heisse _____. (Hello! Mine is _____.)

SPEAKER 1: Sie sprechen Deutsch sehr gut. (You speak German very well.)

SPEAKER 2: Danke schön. Sie sind eine gute Lehrerin. (Thank you. You're a good teacher.)

SPEAKER 1: Danke, ich spreche gerne Deutsch. (Thanks, I like speaking German.)

SPEAKER 2: Auf Wiedersehen! (Goodbye!)

SPEAKER 1: Tschüss! (See you later!)

Spanish

SPEAKER 1: ¡Hola! Me llamo _____. (Hi! My name is _____.)

SPEAKER 2: ¡Hola! Me llamo _____. (Hello! Mine is _____.)

SPEAKER 1: Usted habla muy bien el español. (You speak Spanish very well.)

SPEAKER 2: Gracias. Usted es un buen profesor. (Thank you. You're a good teacher.)

SPEAKER 1: Gracias. Me gusta hablar español. (Thanks. I like speaking Spanish.)

SPEAKER 2: Adiós. (Goodbye.)

SPEAKER 1: Hasta luego. (See you later.)

- Organize a districtwide or citywide Language Week, such as the French Language Week organized in New York City several years ago. Special events, proclamation by the mayor, buttons, stickers, bumper stickers, guest speakers, events at the local universities, etc., all emphasized the French language in the schools and in the universities, for the parents and school administrators and for the general public.

- Enlarge the scope of many of the suggestions listed above under the category of the school and the school community.

- Plan with local associations of teachers of French, Spanish, German, Italian, etc., so that joint efforts can be organized.

- Obtain materials on public relations from ACTFL, the American Council on the Teaching of Foreign Languages, 579 Broadway, Hastings-on-Hudson, N.Y. 10706 and the Northeast Conference, P.O. Box 623, Middlebury, VT 05753. Many state associations of foreign language teachers have materials and slide/sound presentations, videos, etc.

For additional suggestions on publicity and public awareness, see the Bibliography: Bagg *et al.*, 15; De Lopez and Montalvo, 39; Dismuke, 44; and Vidrine, 209.

XI

FLES, FLEX, Immersion Can Be ⸺

FLES/FLEX/immersion can be ⸺. (You fill in the blank!) A program of foreign languages in the elementary school can be:

- unbelievably successful
- all things for all pupils
- FLES, FLEX, immersion, partial immersion
- an exploratory course in language
- an integral part of a sequential program
- a well-coordinated classroom teacher approach
- inexpensive
- an opportunity to enhance the self-image of native speakers of the foreign language
- a custom-tailored program
- a failure if too much is promised for a limited program
- a success, *if* . . .

FLES is a success if the key word is *flexibility* rather than *conformity*. Things should be worked out at the local level so that children are not deprived of a foreign language experience!

FLES is working out well if parents think that their child is learning, their child enjoys the **FLES** class, the time for foreign language is not depriving their child of something else, the **FLES**

175

program gives the school system a good reputation, test scores are outstanding.

FLES is working out well if principals and school administrators think that the foreign language program works smoothly and there are no administrative problems, a reasonable number of the students continue with the foreign language at the middle/junior high school, parents approve of the program, the **FLES** teacher has good rapport with other teachers and students, the **FLES** teacher keeps the class under control and solves behavior problems (if any) at the classroom level, test scores in reading and math are outstanding.

FLES is working out well if classroom teachers think that it is good for their students to learn a foreign language, their students enjoy the foreign language lessons, the **FLES** teacher helps with special projects and holiday activities, the foreign language teacher understands the importance of the rest of the elementary school curriculum, their students are doing well in the foreign language, the foreign language period is scheduled at a convenient time during the school day, test scores are outstanding.

FLES is working out well if the elementary school **FLES** students think that they like the **FLES** teacher, the **FLES** teacher likes them, they understand what is going on, they like the sound of the language, they are praised for doing well, the lessons are not boring, they don't look foolish in front of their friends, they know what is expected of them, it is important to be studying a foreign language, they are not bored with the foreign language activities.

FLES is working out well if secondary school foreign language teachers think that **FLES** supports their program at the secondary school, **FLES** helps to create a positive image for foreign languages, it is good to have colleagues on another level with whom to share ideas and materials, it is important to begin the study of a foreign language in the grades.

FLES can be _____. How will *you* fill in the blank?

Sample Lesson Plans for FLES, FLEX, and Immersion

SAMPLE FLEX LESSON PLAN   (2 languages)

French		Spanish	

I. Opening

    Comment t'appelles tu?　　　¿Cómo te llamas?

II. New presentation—colors

blanc	jaune	blanco	amarillo
rouge	orange	rojo	anaranjado
bleu	noir	azul	negro
vert		verde	

III. Label colors.

    Which colors look similar in French and Spanish?

IV. Game:

    Who can find something in the room that is "rouge"? "rojo"?

    Who is wearing something "vert"? "verde"?

VI. Cultural

    Show flags of Spain and France.

    Which colors are in the French flag?

    Which colors are in the flag of Spain?

VII. Followup

    Find out which colors are in the flags of Canada and Mexico.

NOTES

1. In FLEX in elementary school or exploratory in middle school, there might be a language comparison lesson so that students will begin to see similarities and differences.

2. Future followup lessons would review colors and apply them to new vocabulary about food, clothing, objects in the room, etc.
3. This lesson could be developed in grades 2–3; it also could be expanded to include more reading and some writing for grades 4–6.
4. In grade 6, some social studies applications could be included (e.g., map skills).

LESSON PLAN (FLES, FLEX) FOR GRADES: K, 1, 2

1. Warmup
2. Show me _____ (various objects in the room)
3. Review numbers
4. New work:
   Teach days of the week
   Teach today's date
5. TPR activity
   Go to the chalkboard
           window
           door
           desk
           Marcia's desk
           Richard's chair
6. Review days of the week
7. Sing song

SAMPLE LESSON PLAN, GRADE 5 OR 6 (FLES, FLEX, IMMERSION) Dividing the class into two groups (one group reading; other group skills practice)

1. Warmup (whole class): Review numbers, colors
2. New work (whole class)
   - 2.1 Listening to a story about months of year, seasons
   - 2.2 Repetition of vocabulary
   - 2.3 Question/answer work
3. Group work
   - Group I   Prepare description of pictures
   - Group II   Followup of story
       - Read story
       - Write riddles
       - Do a crossword puzzle
   - Group I   Work with teacher on descriptions
4. Summary (whole class)
   - Group I   Students present descriptions
   - Group II   Students present riddles
5. Find pictures of the four seasons and label them

GUIDELINES FOR GROUP WORK

1. Know students
2. Have a specific purpose
3. Prepare students, space, materials, equipment
4. Arrange the room effectively
5. Train assistants (if available): students, student teachers, etc.
6. Define routines
7. Prepare charts of "More to Do" when students are finished with task
8. Try group work for short periods (first, five minutes)
9. Establish the standards for attention to task

10. Flexibility of groups: group for needs, talents, interest, weaknesses, absence, enrichment, friendship, sociometric indications
11. Evaluate with each group the effectiveness of the session
12. Evaluate with class the effectiveness of the class session

SAMPLE LESSON PLAN FOR FRENCH FLES, IMMERSION (GRADES 4–6)

I. Opening; review of members of the family
II. New presentation (based on the map of the city):
    1. Places on map (La Ville de _____)
    2. Places in the city
    3. Directions: north, south, east, west
    4. Additional places as indicated by question marks
    5. Question/answers: How do I get to _____?
    You go north 3 blocks, turn west . . .
III. Partner practice with the maps
IV. Development of a class dialogue about the map and a fictitious town
(Note: for immersion, this section would be extended to a specific town in France for purposes of teaching geography and historical facts.)
V. Cultural contrasts
    What is the difference between an American market and "l'épicier"? "supermarché"? high school and "lycée"?
VI. Summary of new vocabulary and structures
VII. Followup
    Create your own village with directions for getting from your house to various places in your village.

Next lesson: New presentation of additional places to visit in a town.

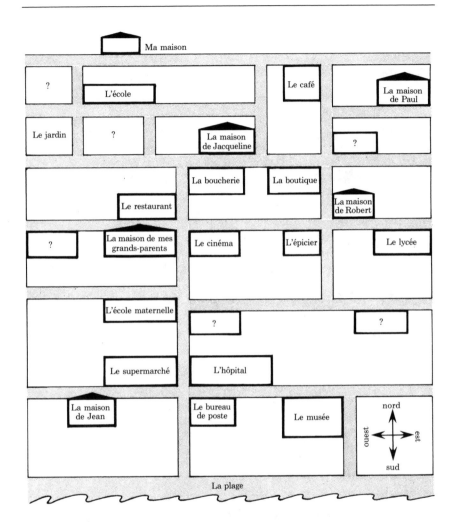

SAMPLE LESSON PLAN FOR SPANISH IMMERSION Social Studies lesson conducted *in Spanish* (Grades 4–6)

I. Map study
   England's location vis-à-vis the New World
   Spain's location vis-à-vis the New World
   France's location vis-à-vis the New World

II. Review of directions
   To go from England to America, Cabot went _____.
   To go from Spain to Mexico, Cortez went _____.
   To go from France to Canada, Cartier went _____.
   To go from Spain to America, Columbus went _____.

III. Discussion of explorers' reasons for coming to America:
   - trade routes
   - spices
   - gold
   - adventure
   - China
   - other reasons

IV. Write a short composition about one of the explorers, explaining why they came, from which country, where they landed, when they landed.

V. Followup
   Role-playing of the adventures of one of the explorers

SAMPLE LESSON PLAN   FLEX (Multilanguage) (Grades 4–6)

I. Introduction to many languages
    Demonstration of places in the world as each "hello" is
    presented and repeated by the class:

Bonjour	France
Buon giorno	(Italy)
Buenos dias	(Spain, Mexico, etc.)
God morgon	(Sweden)
Güten Tag	(Germany
Kalimera	(Greece)
Konnichiwa	(Japan)
Shalom	(Israel)
Zdrastvuytye	(Russia)

II. Design international greeting cards, using some or all of the
     greetings.

III. Followup
     Assignment for students to locate information about
     one or more of the countries concerning:
     location of the country
     type of government
     capital; flag of the country
     name of president, prime minister
     special products from this country
     world-famous people from this country
     other interesting information
     Another assignment might be to create a poem incorpo-
     rating all of these greetings.

APPENDIX **B**

Games for FLES, FLEX, Immersion

INTRODUCTION

Learning a foreign language can be enhanced, enriched, and reinforced by a wide range of approaches and activities. Since youngsters are interested in the new, the exciting, the challenging, the competitive, and the enjoyable, teachers may wish to broaden their repertoire of activities for presenting and for reinforcing foreign language content.

When planning for different types of activities, it should be remembered that

- the emphasis is on some aspect of learning language and culture
- the instructions should be clear and well thought out
- the activity may be used for presentation, for reinforcement, for a change of pace, for review, and even for testing
- the activity should not require elaborate preparation
- the activity should be uncomplicated and permit variations in order to be useful for a number of linguistic concepts
- the classroom climate should be within acceptable limits before, during, and after the activity
- the activity may involve listening, speaking, reading, writing, moving about, gestures, and other types of communication

- for the children, an activity that has a "game" approach is fun; for the teacher it is primarily a learning activity
- if an activity is repeated, it should always have a new twist or surprise
- both the teacher and the children should think that the activity is both worthwhile and fun

There are many types of learning activities that can be used in the FLES, FLEX, or immersion classroom. They can be categorized and grouped, but essentially

- the content of the activity can be varied (one time on clothing, another time on rivers, another time on food)
- if it is a competitive activity, the manner of team composition and scoring can be varied (boys vs. girls, people born in the spring vs. people born in winter, baseball scoring format, etc.).

Bingo-type games (all kinds of activities with cards)

Listening activities

Team games (answering questions of all kinds)

Guessing activities and riddles

TPR activities (such as Simon Says)

Add-on activities

Word activities (such as scrambled sentences, matching, spelling bees)

Number games (such as Buzz and variations)

Wheel games (for numbers, vocabulary, verbs, etc.)

Singing games (for hot or cold)

Charades (for animals, careers)

Prop games (such as Telephone, Restaurant, etc.)

Geography and history games

Board games

Simulations

Problem-solving activities

Any other activities created by teachers and students

SELECTED ACTIVITIES AND GAMES FOR FLES, FLEX, AND IMMERSION

Listening (Grades K, 1, 2)

Tap.   One child taps on the desk, rapidly. Others are called on to tell (in the foreign language) how many taps were heard.

Hello.   One child stands with her/his back to the class. Another child (selected by the teacher) says in the foreign language "Hello, _____. How are you?" The first child replies "Hello. I'm fine. Your name is _____."

Team Games (all levels)

Before/after.   Members of each team are expected to answer, at first, what comes after the picture cue (e.g., picture cue is 21; the answer would be 22). This could be used for days of the week, months, historical events, holidays, etc. Then, children would be asked to answer what comes before. In the sample, the number would be 20. For more advanced classes, children would be asked to say what comes both before and after.

Guessing Games (all levels)

Teacher (or child) would describe a child in the class (hair color, clothing, etc.). The rest of the class guesses who it is.

TPR Games (all levels)

Reverse Simon Says.   Instead of acting on the command of Simon Says, children are expected to follow the command when they *do not* hear "Simon says" and *not* to follow the command when they hear "Simon says."

Charades (professions and careers).   One child is called on to pantomime one of the professions listed on a card she or he has picked. The rest of the class tries to guess the profession or career as acted out by the first child.

What was stolen? Student looks at 15 to 20 articles or pictures of articles displayed on a tray. He or she leaves the room and one item is removed. Student returns and tries to identify the stolen article. Use fewer or more articles depending on the grade level and ability of the class.

Color magic. Teacher agrees with a student helper that the chosen object will be the one immediately after the teacher names a blue object. The class chooses an object, and then the teacher points to a number of objects, asking "Is it the pen?" and so on. The helper knows to say it is the object only when it is the next one after the teacher has pointed out a blue object. Then, colors can be changed in subsequent games.

Group letter. Teacher distributes a sheet of paper to groups of five students. After the first student writes a sentence, she or he folds it over, and then the other students in the group do the same. When all the members of the group have written their sentence, one student reads the sentences to the class. Sometimes they may wish to send these amusing letters to a sick classmate.

It's mine! The student who is It walks around the room and stops near another student and touches an article of clothing or an object on the desk. "It" then says, "It's my (pen)," but does not use the correct name of the object. The student who is seated says "No, it's my (pencil)." If the seated student cannot identify the object correctly, he or she becomes It.

Pin the tail on the _____. A large animal is displayed on a corkboard. The teacher or leader gives various instructions (some of them humorous), and calls on students from each team to do them. There should be a collection of tails, ears, eyes, paws, hats, etc. available.

Memory game. After discussing (in the foreign language) some of the children's food preferences, the teacher then asks "Who likes bananas?" "Who hates string beans?" After several times, the children will listen more carefully and will make an association between the food and the person.

False accusation (grades 5 and 6). The teacher (or a student) prepares cards such as "I went to Paris" or "I went to the bullfight" or "I went to the opera." Students on one team, in turn, guess that Helen went to Paris. Helen, on the opposite team, replies, "Yes, I went to Paris" or "No, I did not go to Paris," according to the card she is holding. The team with the greatest number of correct guesses wins.

Growing, growing (grades 5 and 6).   One student says a word. The next student has to add another word or phrase, and so on, until no one else can say the whole sentence in order to add something else on. This can be played in teams. A variation is to pack a suitcase for a trip, with each child putting something else into the suitcase.

SOURCES FOR ACTIVITIES AND GAMES:

Allen, E., and R. Valette. *Modern Language Classroom Techniques.* New York: Harcourt Brace Jovanovich, 1972, 1977. (2nd ed.)

Danesi, Marcel. *Puzzles and Games in Language Teaching.* Lincolnwood, IL: National Textbook Co., 1986.

Dorry, G. *Games for Second Language Learning.* New York: McGraw-Hill, 1966.

Figueroa, Minerva. *Spanish Resources and Activities.* Lincolnwood, IL: National Textbook Co., 1985.

Finocchiaro, M. *Teaching Children Foreign Languages.* New York: McGraw-Hill, 1964.

Lipton, G. (ed.) *A FLES Sampler: Learning Activities for FLES, FLEX, Immersion.* Champaign, IL: FLES Commission Report to A.A.T.F., 1987.

Macdonald, M., and S. Rogers-Gordon. *Action Plans.* Rowley, MA: Newbury House, 1984.

MacRae, M. *Teaching Spanish in the Grades.* Boston: Houghton-Mifflin, 1960.

Moskowitz, G. *Caring and Sharing in the Foreign Language Class.* Rowley, MA: Newbury House, 1978.

Omaggio, A. *Games and Simulations in the Foreign Language Classroom.* Arlington, VA: Center for Applied Linguistics, 1978.

Sadow, S. *Idea Bank: Creative Activities for the Language Class.* Rowley, MA: Newbury House, 1982.

Schmidt, E. *Let's Play Games in German.* Lincolnwood, IL: National Textbook Co., 1977.

Taylor, M. *Jeux Culturels, Jeux Faciles, Amusons-Nous.* Lincolnwood, IL: National Textbook Co., 1975.

Wright, A., *et al. Games for Language Learning.* Cambridge: Cambridge University Press, 1984. (2nd ed.)

APPENDIX C

Sample Programs

SAMPLE PROGRAM—FLEX
ANNE ARUNDEL COUNTY SCHOOLS, MARYLAND

This program attempts to introduce children to a foreign language (French, German, Russian, Korean, etc.) depending on the background of the volunteers who present the language instruction. The goals are limited, since most sessions meet for approximately one half-hour a week. The volunteers consist of high school students, elementary school classroom teachers, parents, and members of the community.

The program has been in operation since 1978. One of the unique aspects of the program is that the training of the high school student volunteers is handled by the high school chairpersons of foreign languages. There are curriculum bulletins available in French, Spanish, and German for a nominal fee.

Inquiries about the bulletins should be addressed to
Foreign Language Department
Anne Arundel County Public Schools
2644 Riva Rd.
Annapolis, Md. 21401

Since the program is exploratory or introductory in nature, there are few plans for articulation procedures, although many of the students who go through this program are motivated to begin the study of a foreign language in junior high school.

The materials are primarily teacher-made, although the

media departments in the schools have been able to purchase different kinds of foreign language materials.

A parent said of the program "The elementary school age children have an enthusiasm to learn, and they are made aware of language expressions and customs, family life-styles, history, art, and cultures of other children in the world."

SAMPLE PROGRAM—SEQUENTIAL FLES HINSDALE ELEMENTARY SCHOOLS, ILLINOIS

This program has been in operation since 1960, and is unique because there is a foreign language continuum from grade 5 through grade 12. All the teachers are certified as language teachers, which accounts for the strength and longevity of the program.

The time schedule varies from grade to grade: 20 minutes a day in the 5th grade; 30 minutes a day in the 6th grade. These students move on to the junior high school program (45 minutes) in grades 7 and 8.

Most of the grade 5 students choose either the French or Spanish program. It is remarkable that close to 90 percent of the eligible 7th graders continue their study of the same foreign language. The articulation of the elementary school program is accomplished successfully because teachers are assigned to teach on both the elementary and junior high school levels. There is a course of study, and inquiries should be addressed to

Foreign Language Coordinator
Hinsdale Public Schools
Hinsdale, Illinois

The coordinator said of the program "The premise in this district is that foreign language study is an advantage in any number of ways—as a career booster, in the transfer of learning, and as a vital ingredient in a good basic education."

Other programs of this type are those in Hunter College Elementary School and other schools in New York City, Chicago, Louisiana, Glastonbury, Conn., Baltimore, Md., and Dobbs Ferry, N.Y., just to mention a few. Many others are beginning throughout the country.

SAMPLE PROGRAM—IMMERSION
MILWAUKEE PUBLIC SCHOOLS,
MILWAUKEE, WISCONSIN

This program is a total immersion program, for children in kindergarten through grade 6, in French, German, and Spanish. The goals are more ambitious than either FLEX or FLES, so that by the end of grade 6, students will achieve a level of proficiency in English and the second language such that "they are able to pursue their studies with ease in both languages."

Teachers are certified for elementary school instruction, with proficiency in a second language. They follow the standard curriculum for elementary schools.

There are two unique features of the program. The first is that there are no selection criteria for students to enter the program. The second is that students from the immersion elementary schools go to an immersion middle school in grades 7 and 8. This successful solution to the problem of articulation is an outstanding accomplishment.

The results on standardized tests indicate that students in the immersion program are achieving at or above ability level, and their test scores show improvement grade by grade.

The goal is based on the learning activity (reading, mathematics, social studies, etc.), not the language, but the achievement in language is an extra benefit.

The curriculum covers the Milwaukee elementary school curriculum. Inquiries should be addressed to

Foreign Language Curriculum Specialist
Milwaukee Public Schools
P.O. Drawer 10K
Milwaukee, Wisconsin 53201-8210

Other programs of this type include Montgomery County, Md., Cincinnati, Ohio, Culver City, Cal., San Diego, Cal., and Holliston, Mass., to mention a few. Many others are beginning throughout the country.

APPENDIX D

Selected Bibliography

1. Alcorn, C. "College Language Students in the Elementary School Classroom." *Language Association Bulletin* 37 (Jan. 1987): 9–10.
2. Alexander, L., and M. John. "Testing Oral Skills in a FLES Short Course." *Foreign Language Annals* 18 (Nov. 1985): 235–39.
3. Allen, E., and R. Valette. *Modern Language Classroom Techniques.* New York: Harcourt Brace Jovanovich, 1972, 1977. (2nd ed.)
4. Allen, V. "If Reading—How?" pp. 53–60, in R. Freudenstein (ed.), *Teaching Foreign Languages to the Very Young.* Oxford: Pergamon Press, 1979.
5. Anderson, H., and C. Pesola. *Language and Children: Making the Match.* Reading, MA: Addison-Wesley, forthcoming.
6. Anderson, H., and N. Rhodes. "Immersion and Other Innovations in the U.S. Elementary Schools," pp. 167–81, in S. Savignon and M. Berns (eds.), *Initiatives in Communicative Language Teaching.* Reading, MA: Addison-Wesley, 1984.
7. Andersson, T. *A Guide to Family Reading in Two Languages: the Preschool Years.* Roslyn, VA: National Clearinghouse for Bilingual Education, 1981.
8. Andersson, T. "Parents, Wake Up! Why Deprive Your Child of a Superior Education?" *Hispania* 63 (May 1980): 391–93.
9. Andersson, T. *Foreign Language in the Elementary School: A Struggle against Mediocrity.* Austin: University of Texas Press, 1969.
10. Angiolillo, P. "French for the Feebleminded: An Experiment." *Modern Language Journal* 26 (April 1942): 266–71.

11. Asher, J. *Learning Another Language through Actions*. Los Gatos, CA: Sky Oakes Publications, 1979, 1982. (2nd ed.)

12. Asher, J., and R. García. "The Optimal Age to Learn a Foreign Language," pp. 3–12, in S. Krashen and others (eds.), *Child-Adult Differences in Second Language Acquisition*. Rowley, MA: Newbury House, 1982.

13. Aspel, P. "Wednesday 10:00 A.M., 1987," pp. 153–67, in G. Lipton (ed.), *Projections into the Future*, FLES Report to A.A.T.F., 1968.

14. Astley, H. *Get the Message*. Cambridge: Cambridge University Press, 1985.

15. Bagg, G., M. Oates , and G. Zucker. "Building Community Support through a Spanish FLES Program." *Hispania* 67 (Mar. 1984): 105–8.

16. Balanz, L., and W. Teetor. *German for Elementary Schools*. Albany, NY: N.Y. State Education Department, 1970.

17. Baranick, W., and P. Markham. "Attitudes of Elementary School Principals toward Foreign Language Instruction." *Foreign Language Annals* 19 (Dec. 1986): 481–89.

18. Barnett, H. "Foreign Languages for Younger Students and Foreign Languages for ALL Students: A Perfect Marriage." *Language Association Bulletin* (Jan. 1986): 5.

19. Barnett, H. "Peer Teaching: FLES Programs." *Hispania* 56 (Sept. 1973): 635–38.

20. Barnett, H. "Let's Harness FLES Enthusiasm." *Hispania* 53 (Dec. 1970): 979–82.

21. Bartz, W. *Testing Oral Communication in the Foreign Language Classroom*. Washington, D.C.: Center for Applied Linguistics, 1979.

22. *Bellevue Spanish Immersion Program: A Description for Parents*. Bellevue, WA: Bellevue Public Schools, 1987.

23. Birckbichler, D. *Creative Activities for the Second Language Classroom*. Washington, D.C.: Center for Applied Linguistics, 1982.

24. Birckbichler, D., and A. Omaggio. "Diagnosing and Responding to Individual Learner Needs." *Modern Language Journal* 62 (Nov. 1978): 336–45.

25. Bourque, J., and L. Chehy. "Exploratory Language and Culture: A Unique Program." *Foreign Language Annals* 9 (Feb. 1976): 10–16.

26. Bragaw, D., H. Zimmer-Loew, *et al.* "Social Studies and Foreign Languages: A Partnership," *Social Education* (Feb. 1985): 92–96.

27. Brega, E., and J. Newell. "H.S. Performance of FLES and non-FLES Students." *Modern Language Journal* 51 (Nov. 1967): 408–11.

28. Brooks, N. *Language and Language Learning*. New York: Harcourt, Brace and World, 1964.

29. Buckby, M. "Is Primary Foreign Language Really in the Balance?" *Modern Language Journal* 60 (Nov. 1976): 340–46.

30. Campbell, R., T. Gray, *et al.* "Foreign Language Learning in the Elementary Schools: A Comparison of Three Language Programs." *Modern Language Journal* 69 (Spring 1985): 44–54.

31. Carroll, J. "Foreign Language Proficiency Levels Attained by Language Majors near Graduation from College." *Foreign Language Annals* 1 (Dec. 1967): 131–35.

32. Carroll, J. "Foreign Languages for Children: What Research Says." *National Elementary Principal* 39 (May 1960): 12–15

33. Chase, C. "An Hispanic Tale for the Second Language Elementary Classroom." *Hispania* 69 (May 1986): 395–98.

34. Cohen, A. "The Culver City Spanish Immersion Program." *Modern Language Journal* 58 (Mar. 1974): 95–103.

35. Collet, E. "Teaching French to the Very Young." *A.A.T.F. National Bulletin* 12 (Jan. 1987): 8.

36. Curtain, H. "The Immersion Approach: Principle and Practice," pp. 1–14, in B. Snyder (ed.), *Second Language Acquisition: Preparing for Tomorrow*. Lincolnwood, IL: National Textbook Co., 1986.

37. Damen, L. *Culture Learning: The Fifth Dimension in the Language Classroom*. Reading, MA: Addison-Wesley, 1987.

38. Dammer, P., *et al.* "FLES: A Guide for Program Review." *Modern Language Journal* 52 (Jan. 1968): 15–25.

39. De Lopez, M., and M. Montalvo. "Developing Public Support for Community Language Programs: A Working Model." *Foreign Language Annals* 19 (Sept. 1986): 529–31.

40. DeLorenzo, W., and L. Gladstein. "Immersion Education à l'Américaine: A Descriptive Study of U.S. Immersion Programs." *Foreign Language Annals* 17 (Nov. 1984): 35–40.

41. Derrick, W., and R. Khorshed. "Early Immersion in French." *Today's Education* (Feb.–Mar. 1979): 38–40.

42. De Sauze, E. *The Cleveland Plan for the Teaching of Modern Languages*. Philadelphia: Winston Co., 1929.

43. Di Pietro, R. "Filling the Elementary School Curriculum with Languages: What Are the Effects?" *Foreign Language Annals* 13 (April 1980): 115–23.

44. Dismuke, D. "Learning Foreign Languages Is 'In' at All Levels." *NEA Today* 5 (April 1987): 4–5.
45. Donoghue, M. "Recent Research in FLES (1974–1980)." *Hispania* 64 (Dec. 1981): 602–4.
46. Donoghue, M., and J. Kunkle. *Second Languages in Primary Education.* Rowley, MA: Newbury House, 1979.
47. Donoghue, M. "Presenting the Cultural Component during FLES." *Hispania* 61 (Mar. 1978): 124–26.
48. Donoghue, M. *Foreign Languages and the Elementary School Child.* Dubuque, IA: William C. Brown, 1968.
49. Dufort, M. "Foreign Language Attitude Scale," pp. 71–73, in R. Politzer and L. Weiss (eds.), *The Successful Foreign Language Teacher.* Philadelphia: Center for Curriculum Development, 1969.
50. Dulay, H., M. Burt, and S. Krashen. *Language Two.* New York: Oxford University Press, 1982.
51. Dunkel, H., and R. Pillet. *French in the Elementary School.* Chicago: University of Chicago Press, 1962.
52. Dunlea, A. *How Do We Learn Languages?* Cambridge: Cambridge University Press, 1985.
53. Eddy, P. "Foreign Language in the USA: A National Survey of American Attitudes and Experience." *Modern Language Journal* 64 (Spring 1980): 58–63.
54. Ehrlich, M. "Parents: The Child's Most Important Teachers," pp. 97–110, in J. Darcy (ed.), *The Language Teacher: Commitment and Collaboration.* Middlebury, VT: The Northeast Conference on the Teaching of Foreign Languages, 1987.
55. "Elementary School Foreign Language," pp. 11–23, in R. Mead (ed.), *Foreign Languages: Key Links in the Chain in Learning.* Middlebury, VT: The Northeast Conference on the Teaching of Foreign Languages, 1983.
56. *Everything You Always Wanted to Know about Foreign Languages: A Handbook on How to Be a Successful Foreign Language Student.* Annapolis, MD: Anne Arundel County Schools, 1981.
57. Fathman, A. "The Relationship between Age and Second Language Productive Ability," pp. 115–22, in S. Krashen, *et al.* (eds.), *Child-Adult Differences in Second Language Acquisition.* Rowley, MA: Newbury House, 1982.
58. Feindler, J. "What Ever Happened to the Joy of Foreign Language Teaching?" *Language Association Bulletin* 32 (May 1981): 10.
59. Finocchiaro, M. *Teaching Children Foreign Languages.* New York: McGraw-Hill, 1964.

60. Fiske, E. "Foreign Languages in Early Grades." *Baltimore Sun*, June 10, 1983.

61. Flaitz, J. "Building the Basic Skills through Foreign Language in the Elementary School." *Language Association Bulletin* 24 (May 1983): 1–3.

62. Forsythe, T. "Soaking It Up in Milwaukee." *American Education* 17 (July 1980): 21–25.

63. *French Achievement Test*. New York: Gifted Child Project, New York City Board of Education, 1970.

64. *French in the Elementary School*. New York: New York City Board of Education, 1963.

65. Freudenstein, R. (ed.) *Teaching Foreign Languages to the Very Young*. Oxford: Pergamon Press, 1979.

66. Garnett, N. "Establishing a Primary Level School of Spanish." *Hispania* 70 (Mar. 1987): 167–70.

67. Gass, S., and C. Madden (eds.) *Input in Second Language Acquisition*. Rowley, MA: Newbury House, 1985.

68. Genesee, F. *Learning through Two Languages*. Rowley, MA: Newbury House, 1987.

69. Genesee, F. "Acquisition of Reading Skills in Immersion Programs." *Foreign Language Annals* 12 (Feb. 1979): 71–77.

70. Genesee, F. "The Suitability of Immersion Programs for All Children." *Canadian Modern Language Review* 32 (May 1976): 494–515.

71. Ginsburg, H., and I. McCoy. "An Empirical Rationale for Foreign Languages in Elementary School." *Modern Language Journal* 65 (Spring 1981): 36–42.

72. Gradisnik, A. "Television Can Be Effective in the FLES Program . . . If." *Hispania* 49 (Sept. 1966): 485–89.

73. Gramer, V. "Hinsdale, Illinois, FLES Program," pp. 35–48, in G. Lipton, *et al* (eds.), *The Many Faces of FLES*. Champaign, IL: FLES Commission Report to A.A.T.F., 1985.

74. Gray, T., N. Rhodes, *et al. Comparative Evaluation of Elementary School Foreign Language Programs. Final Report*. Washington, D.C.: Center for Applied Linguistics, 1984.

75. Green, J. "Hello World!" *Instructor* 89 (Oct. 1979): 91–94.

76. Griffin, R. "Using Current Magazines as a Resource for Teaching Culture." *Hispania* 70 (May 1987): 400–2.

77. Hancock, C., G. Lipton, *et al.* "A Study of FLES and non-FLES Pupils' Attitudes toward the French and Their Culture." *French Review* 49 (April 1976): 717–22.

78. Harding, E., and P. Riley. *The Bilingual Family: A Handbook for*

Parents. Cambridge: Cambridge University Press, 1986.

79. Hawley, D., and M. Oates. "FLES Certification for Secondary Teachers: An Idea Whose Time Has Come." *Iowa FLES Newletter* 1:2 (Spring 1985): 4–5.

80. Hayden, R. "A Beginning: Building Global Competence." *State Education Leader* 2 (Fall 1983): 1–3.

81. Higgs, T. (ed.) *Teaching for Proficiency, the Organizing Principle.* Lincolnwood, IL: National Textbook Co., 1984.

82. Hornby, P. "Achieving Second Language Fluency through Immersion Education." *Foreign Language Annals* 13 (Apr. 1980): 107–12.

83. Howe, E. "The Success of the Cherry Hill Spanish Immersion Program in Orem, Utah." *Hispania* 66 (Dec. 1983): 592–97.

84. Hunter, M. "Individualizing FLES." *Hispania* 57 (Sept. 1974): 494–97.

85. Hunter, M. *Teach More—Faster.* El Segundo, CA: TIP Publications, 1969.

86. Jacobs, G. "An American FL Immersion Program: How To." *Foreign Language Annals* 11 (Sept. 1978): 405–13.

87. Jarvis, G. (ed.) *The Challenge for Excellence in Foreign Language Education.* Middlebury, VT: The Northeast Conference on the Teaching of Foreign Languages, 1984.

88. Johnson, S., and C. Johnson. *The One Minute Teacher.* New York: William Morrow and Co., 1986.

89. Joiner, E. "Evaluating the Cultural Component of FL Tests." *Modern Language Journal* 58 (Sept. 1974): 242–44.

90. Jones, K. *Simulations in Language Teaching.* Cambridge: Cambridge University Press, 1982.

91. Kennedy, D., and W. DeLorenzo. *Complete Guide to Exploratory Foreign Language Programs.* Lincolnwood, IL: National Textbook Co., 1985.

92. Koster, C. "English FLES in the Netherlands: How Good Must a Teacher Be?" *Modern Language Journal* 70 (Spring 1986): 8–12.

93. Krashen, S. "Immersion: Why It Works and What It Has Taught Us." *Language and Society* 12 (Winter 1984): 61–64.

94. Krashen, S. *Principles and Practice in Second Language Acquisition.* Oxford: Pergamon Press, 1983.

95. Krashen, S., and T. Terrell. *The Natural Approach to Language Acquisition in the Classroom.* Oxford: Pergamon Press, 1983.

96. Krashen, S., M. Long, *et al.* (eds.) *Child-Adult Differences in Second Language Acquisition.* Rowley, MA: Newbury House, 1982.

97. Kunkle, J., and A. Cipriani (eds.) *Foreign Language Teaching Techniques in FLES and Bilingual Settings.* FLES Report to A.A.T.F., 1973.

98. Kunkle, J. "Now that FLES Is Dead, What Next?" *Educational Leadership* 79 (Feb. 1972): 417–19.

99. Lambert, W., and G. Tucker. *Bilingual Education of Children: The St. Lambert Experiment.* Rowley, MA: Newbury House, 1972.

100. Landry, R. "A Comparison of Second Language Learners and Monolinguals on Divergent Thinking Tasks at the Elementary School Level." *Modern Language Journal* 58 (Jan. 1974): 10–15.

101. Landry, R. "The Enhancement of Figural Creativity through Second Language Learning at the Elementary School Level." *Foreign Language Annals* 7 (Oct. 1973): 111–15.

102. Larew, L. "After Second Language Immersion–What?" *Language Association Bulletin* 38 (Mar. 1987): 26.

103. Larew, L. "The Teacher of FLES in 1986." *Hispania* (Sept. 1986): 699–701.

104. Lee, W. "For and Against an Early Start." *Foreign Language Annals* 10 (Mar. 1977): 263–70.

105. Lenneberg, E. *Biological Foundations of Language.* New York: John Wiley, 1967.

106. Levenson, S., and W. Kendrick. *Readings in Foreign Languages for the Elementary Schools.* Waltham, MA: Blaisdell, 1967.

107. Lipton, G. (ed.) *A FLES Sampler: Learning Activities for FLES, FLEX, Immersion.* Champaign, IL: FLES Commission Report to A.A.T.F., 1987.

108. Lipton, G. "They Love Foreign Languages for Children," in K. Muller (ed.), *Children and Languages: Research and Practice in the Elementary Grades.* New York: National Council on Foreign Languages and International Studies, 1987 (forthcoming).

109. Lipton, G., N. Rhodes, and H. Curtain (eds.) *The Many Faces of Foreign Language in the Elementary School: FLES, FLEX and Immersion.* Champaign, IL: FLES Commission Report to A.A.T.F., 1985.

110. Lipton, G. *Yes to Lex, or Elementary School FL Instruction Helps English Language Skills: Results of a Pilot Study.* Unpublished paper, available from author, 1979.

111. Lipton, G. "FLES Can Be . . ." Speech Delivered at Annual Meeting of the New York State Association of Foreign Language Teachers, 1974.

112. Lipton, G., and E. Bourque (eds.) *FLES USA: Success Stories*. FLES Report to A.A.T.F., 1972.

113. Lipton, G., and W. Teetor. *Why FLES?* Schenectady, NY: New York State Association of Foreign Language Teachers, 1972.

114. Lipton, G., and V. Spaar-Rauch (eds.) *FLES Goals and Guides*. FLES Report to A.A.T.F., 1971.

115. Lipton, G. "A Potpouri of Ideas for French FLES Classes." *Instructor* 80 (Jan. 1971): 49–53.

116. Lipton, G., and J. Mirsky. *Spanish for Elementary Schools*. Albany, NY: New York State Department of Education, 1970.

117. Lipton, G., and V. Spaar-Rauch (eds.) *FLES: Patterns for Change*. FLES Report to A.A.T.F., 1970.

118. Lipton, G., and E. Bourque (eds.) *The 3 R's of FLES*. FLES Report to A.A.T.F., 1969.

119. Lipton, G. "The Effectiveness of Listening-Speaking-Only, as Compared with Listening-Speaking-Reading in Grade Four, the First Year of Study of French at the FLES Level, in the Acquisition of Auditory Comprehension." Doctoral Dissertation, New York University, 1969. Dissertation Abstracts International, 30/06-A, 2421.

120. Lipton, G. "To Read or Not to Read: An Experiment on the FLES Level." *Foreign Language Annals* 3 (Dec. 1969): 241–46.

121. Lipton, G. (ed.) *FLES Projections into the Future*. FLES Report to A.A.T.F., 1969.

122. Lipton, G, and N. Alkonis. *French for Elementary Schools*. Albany, NY: New York State Education Department, 1966.

123. Lipton, G. "Welcome to FLES!" *French Review* 38 (Dec. 1964): 229–32.

124. Littlewood, W. *Foreign and Second Language Learning*. Cambridge: Cambridge University Press, 1984.

125. Littlewood, W. *Communicative Language Teaching: An Introduction*. Cambridge: Cambridge University Press, 1981.

126. Lopato, E. "FLES and Academic Achievement." *French Review* 36 (1965): 499–507.

127. Love, F., and L. Honig. *Options and Perspectives: A Sourcebook of Innovative Foreign Language Programs in Action, K–12*. New York: Modern Language Association, 1973.

128. Lundin, J., and D. Dolson (eds.) *Studies on Immersion Education: A Collection for U.S. Educators*. Sacramento, CA: California State Department of Education, Office of Bilingual Bicultural Education, 1984.

129. Macdonald, M., and S. Rogers-Gordon. *Action Plans*. Rowley, MA: Newbury House, 1984.

130. MacRae, M. *Teaching Spanish in the Grades*. Boston: Houghton-Mifflin, 1960.
131. Maley, A., and A. Duff. *Drama Techniques in Language Learning*. Cambridge: Cambridge University Press, 1978, 1982 (2nd ed.).
132. Maley, A., and A. Duff. *Sounds Intriguing*. Cambridge: Cambridge University Press, 1979.
133. Maley, A., and A. Duff. *Variations on a Theme*. Cambridge: Cambridge University Press, 1978.
134. Maley, A., and A. Duff. *Sounds Interesting*. Cambridge: Cambridge University Press, 1975.
135. Masciantonio, R. "Tangible Benefits of the Study of Latin: A Review of Research." *Foreign Language Annals* 10 (Sept. 1977): 375–82.
136. Mavrogenes, N. "Latin in Elementary School, A Help for Reading and Language Arts." *Phi Delta Kappan* 60 (May 1979): 675–77.
137. Mazziotti, J. *Active Vocabulary Building*. Schenectady, NY: New York State Association of Foreign Language Teachers, 1985.
138. McKim, L. *FLES: Types of Programs*. ERIC Focus Reports, No. 16. New York: American Council on the Teaching of Foreign Languages, 1970.
139. McLaughlin, B. "Are Immersion Programs the Answer for Bilingual Education in the U.S.?" *Bilingual Review* 11 (Jan./Apr. 1984): 3–10.
140. McLaughlin, B. *Children's Second Language Learning*. Washington, D.C.: Center for Applied Linguistics, 1982.
141. Met, M. "Twenty Questions: The Most Commonly Asked Questions about Starting an Immersion Program.". *Foreign Language Annals* (forthcoming).
142. Met, M. "Decisions! Decisions! Decisions! Foreign Language in the Elementary School." *Foreign Language Annals* 18 (Dec. 1985): 469–73.
143. Met, M. "Listening Comprehension and the Young Second Language Learner." *Foreign Language Annals* 17 (Oct. 1984): 519–23.
144. Met, M. "The Rebirth of Foreign Languages in the Elementary School." *Educational Leadership* 37 (Jan. 1980): 321–23.
145. Montessori, M. *The Secret of Childhood*. New York: Ballantine Books, 1966.
146. Moskowitz, G. *Caring and Sharing in the Foreign Language Class*. Rowley, MA: Newbury House, 1978.
147. Moskowitz, G. "Competency Based Teacher Education: Before

We Proceed." *Modern Language Journal* 60 (Jan. 1976): 18–23.

148. Muller, K. (ed.) *Children and Languages: Research and Practice in the Elementary Grades.* New York: National Council on Foreign Languages and International Studies, 1987 (forthcoming).

149. Nessel, D. "Reading Comprehension: Asking the Right Questions." *Phi Delta Kappan* 68 (Feb. 1987): 442–45.

150. "Notes on FLES Certification in Kansas." *Iowa FLES Newsletter* (Fall 1986): 1, 5.

151. Oates, M. "A Non-Intensive FLES Program in French." *French Review* 54 (Mar. 1980): 507–13.

152. Oller, J., and K. Perkins (eds.) *Research in Language Testing.* Rowley, MA: Newbury House, 1980.

153. Omaggio, A. *Teaching Language in Context.* Boston: Heinle and Heinle, 1986.

154. Omaggio, A. *Proficiency-Oriented Classroom Testing.* Washington, D.C.: Center for Applied Linguistics, 1983.

155. Omaggio, A. *Helping Learners Succeed: Activities for the Foreign Language Classroom.* Washington, D.C.: Center for Applied Linguistics, 1981.

156. Omaggio, A. *Games and Simulations in the Foreign Language Classroom.* Arlington, VA: Center for Applied Linguistics, 1978.

157. Oneto, A. *FLES Evaluation: Language Skills and Pupil Attitudes in Fairfield Connecticut Public Schools.* Hartford, CT: Connecticut State Department of Education, 1967.

158. Ozete, O. "Milwaukee's French, German, Spanish Immersion Success." *Hispania* 63 (Dec. 1980): 569–71.

159. Paananen, D. "Why Your Youngster Should Learn a Foreign Language." *Better Homes and Gardens* (Oct. 1981): 17–19.

160. Papalia, A. "A Synthesis on What Research Says on Early Second Language Learning." *Language Association Bulletin* 37 (Jan. 1986): 11–14.

161. Paquette, F. (ed.) *New Dimensions in the Teaching of FLES.* Bloomington, IN: Indiana Language Project, 1968.

162. Penfield, W. "The Learning of Languages," pp. 192–214, in J. Michel (ed.) *Foreign Language Teaching Today.* New York: Macmillan, 1967.

163. Penfield, W., and L. Roberts. *Speech and Brain Mechanisms.* New York: Atheneum Press, 1959.

164. Pesola, C. *A Source Book for Elementary and Middle School Language Programs.* Minneapolis: Minnesota State Department of Education, 1982.

165. Pfaff, C. (ed.) *First and Second Language Acquisition Process.* Cambridge, MA: Newbury House, 1987.

166. Rafferty, E. *Second Language Study and Basic Skills in Louisiana.* Baton Rouge, LA: Louisiana Department of Education, 1986.

167. Rhodes, N., and M. Snow. "Foreign Language in the Elementary School: A Comparison of Achievement." *ERIC/CLL News Bulletin* 7 (Mar. 1984): 3–5.

168. Rhodes, N. "FLES: Are Languages Making a Comeback?" *Principal* 62 (Mar. 1983): 24–28.

169. Rhodes, N., and A. Schreibstein. *Foreign Language in the Elementary School: A Practical Guide.* Washington, D.C.: Center for Applied Linguistics, 1983.

170. Rhodes, N., *et al. Elementary School Foreign Language Instruction in the U.S.: Innovative Approaches for the 1980's. Final Report.* Washington, D.C.: Center for Applied Linguistics, 1981.

171. Rivers, W. *Communicating Naturally in a Second Language.* Cambridge: Cambridge University Press, 1983.

172. Roberts, F. "Should Your Child Learn a Foreign Language?" *Parents' Magazine* 61 (April 1986): 58–62.

173. Rosenbusch, M. "FLES: An Important Step in the Right Direction." *Hispania* 68 (Mar. 1985): 174–76.

174. Sadow, S. *Idea Bank: Creative Activities for the Language Class.* Rowley, MA: Newbury House, 1982.

175. Savignon, S., and M. Berns (eds.) *Initiatives in Communicative Language Teaching.* Reading, MA: Addison-Wesley, 1984.

176. Savignon, S. *Communicative Competence: Theory and Classroom and Classroom Practice.* Reading, MA: Addison-Wesley, 1983.

177. Scarcella, R., and C. Higa. "Input and Age Differences in Second Language Acquisition," pp. 175-201 in S. Krashen, *et al. Child-Adult Differences in Second Language Acquisition.* Rowley, MA: Newbury House, 1982.

178. Schinko-Llano, L. *Foreign Language in the Elementary School: State of the Art.* Washington, D.C.: Center for Applied Linguistics, 1985.

179. Schneider, J. "PTA and TPR: A Comprehension-Based Approach in a Public Elementary School." *Hispania* 67 (Dec. 1984): 620–25.

180. Schrade, A. "Des Plaines FLES: Successful Language Arts and Social Studies Integration." 61 *Hispania* (Sept. 1978): 504–7.

181. Seefeldt, C., and N. Barbour. *Early Childhood Education.* Columbus, OH: Merrill, 1986.

182. Seelye, H. *Teaching Culture*. Lincolnwood, IL: National Textbook Co., 1983.

183. Segal, Be. *Enseñando el español por medio de acción*. Brea, CA: Berty Segal, Inc., 1982.

184. Sheperd, G., and W. Ragan. *Modern Elementary Curriculum*. New York: Holt, Rinehart and Winston, 1982.

185. Simon, P. *The Tongue-Tied American*. New York: Continuum, 1980.

186. Sims, W., and S. Hammond. *Award-Winning Foreign Language Programs: Prescriptions for Success*. Lincolnwood, IL: National Textbook Co., 1981.

187. Smith, S. *The Theatre Arts and the Teaching of Second Languages*. Reading, MA: Addison-Wesley, 1984.

188. *Somerville, N.J., Public Schools Report on FLES*. Somerville: Board of Education, 1962.

189. *Spanish in Elementary Schools*. New York: Board of Education, 1963.

190. Sparkman, L. (ed.) *Culture in the FLES Program*. Philadelphia: Chilton, 1966.

191. Spilka, I. "Assessment of Second-Language Performance in Immersion Programs." *Canadian Modern Language Review* 32 (May 1976): 543–61.

192. Stanislawczyk, I., and S. Yavner. *Creativity in the Language Classroom*. Rowley, MA: Newbury House, 1976.

193. Stern, H. "The Immersion Phenomenon." *Language and Society* 12 (Winter 1984): 4–6.

194. Stern, H. "Toward a Multidimensional Foreign Language Curriculum," pp. 120–46, in R. Mead, (ed.) *Foreign Languages: Key Links in the Chain in Learning*. Middlebury, VT: The Northeast Conference on the Teaching of Foreign Languages, 1983.

195. Stern, H. "Optimal Age: Myth or Reality?" *Canadian Modern Language Review* 32 (Feb. 1976): 283–94.

196. Stern, H. *Foreign Languages in Primary Education*. Paris: UNESCO, 1963.

197. Sternberg, R. "Teaching Critical Thinking: Eight Easy Ways to Fail Before You Begin." *Phi Delta Kappan* 68 (Feb. 1987): 45–9.

198. Stevens, F. *Strategies for Second Language Acquisition*. Montreal: Eden Press, 1984.

199. Stevick, E. *Images and Options in the Language Classroom*. Cambridge: Cambridge University Press, 1986.

200. Stevick, E. *Teaching and Learning Language*. Cambridge:

Cambridge University Press, 1982.

201. Stevick, E. *Memory, Meaning, Method: Some Psychological Perspectives in Language Learning.* Rowley, MA: Newbury House, 1976.

202. Stewart, P. "From the President. . . ." *A.A.T.F. National Bulletin* 12 (April 1987): 1.

203. Swain, M. "Communicative Competence: Some Roles of Comprehensible Input and Comprehensible Output in Its Development," pp. 257–71, in S. Gass and C. Madden (eds.) *Input in Second Language Acquisition.* Rowley, MA: Newbury House, 1985.

204. *Total and Partial Immersion Language Programs in the U.S. Elementary Schools.* Washington, D.C.: Center for Applied Linguistics, 1987.

205. Trites, R. *Primary French Immersion: Disabilities and Prediction of Success.* Toronto: OISE Press, 1981.

206. Tuttle, H. "Mnemonics in Spanish Classes." *Hispania* 64 (Dec. 1981): 572–74.

207. Ur, P. *Teaching Listening Comprehension.* Cambridge: Cambridge University Press, 1984.

208. Valette, R. *Modern Language Testing.* New York: Harcourt, Brace, Jovanovich, 1977. (2nd ed.)

209. Vidrine, D. "The Fête Française: A Promotional Venture." *Foreign Language Annals* 19 (Sept. 1986): 305–10.

210. Vines, L. *A Guide to Language Camps in the U.S.* Washington, D.C.: ERIC Clearinghouse on Languages and Linguistics, 1983.

211. Vobejda, B. "U.S. Students Called Internationally Illiterate." *Washington Post*, Nov. 22, 1986, A-7.

212. Vocolo, J. "The Effect of Foreign Language Study in Elementary School upon Achievement in the Same FL in High School." *Modern Language Journal* 51 (Dec. 1967): 463–70.

213. Wallace, N. "The Early Second Language Experience." *Language Association Bulletin* 37 (Jan. 1986): 1–4.

214. Wallace, N., and C. Wirth. *Vocabulary Building and Cultural Activities for Early Second Language Programs.* Schenectady, NY: New York State Association of Foreign Language Teachers, 1985.

215. Wasserman, S. "Teaching for Thinking: Louis E. Raths Revisited." *Phi Delta Kappan* 68 (Feb. 1987): 460–65.

216. Weeks, T. *Born to Talk.* Rowley, MA: Newbury House, 1979.

217. *What Works.* Washington, D.C.: U.S. Department of Education, 1986.

218. Wilson, V., and B. Wattenmaker. *Real Communication in Foreign*

Languages. Boston, MA: Allyn and Bacon, 1980.

219. Wing, B. (ed.) *Listening, Reading, Writing: Analysis and Application.* Middlebury, VT: The Northeast Conference on the Teaching of Foreign Languages, 1986.

220. Wing, B. "For Teachers: A Challenge for Competence," pp. 11–46, in G. Jarvis. (ed.), *The Challenge of Excellence in Foreign Language Education.* Middlebury, VT: The Northeast Conference on the Teaching of Foreign Languages, 1984.

221. Wright, A., *et al. Games for Language Learning.* Cambridge: Cambridge University Press, 1984. (2nd ed.)

About the Author

DR. GLADYS LIPTON is one of the leading authorities on Foreign Languages in the Elementary School (FLES). She has directed K–12 foreign language programs in the New York City and the Anne Arundel, Maryland, school systems. Having served as a consultant for bilingual and immersion schools, and as a FLES methods course instructor at Brooklyn College (New York) and the University of Maryland/ Baltimore County, she is frequently in demand as a workshop presenter and keynote speaker.

Dr. Lipton has taught foreign languages on all school levels, and has published widely in such publications as, *Hispania, French Review, Instructor magazine, Inside Education,* and *Handbook of the American Association of School Administrators.* She currently serves as the Chair of the National FLES/FLEX/Immersion Commission of A.A.T.F., which offers assistance on FLES nationally. As the Coordinator of Foreign Language Workshops for the Department of Modern Languages and Linguistics at the University of Maryland/Baltimore County, she coordinates outreach immersion programs for both teachers and students, and directs a language camp for elementary school youngsters at the university.

NTC PROFESSIONAL MATERIALS

ACTFL Review
Published annually in conjunction with the American Council on the Teaching of Foreign Languages

Modern Media in Foreign Language Education: Theory and Implementation, *ed. Smith*, Vol. 18 (1987)

Defining and Developing Proficiency: Guidelines, Implementations, and Concepts, *ed. Byrnes*, Vol. 17 (1986)

Foreign Language Proficiency in the Classroom and Beyond, *ed. James*, Vol. 16 (1984)

Teaching for Proficiency, the Organizing Principle, *ed. Higgs*, Vol. 15 (1983)

Practical Applications of Research in Foreign Language Teaching, *ed. James*, Vol. 14 (1982)

Curriculum, Competence, and the Foreign Language Teacher, *ed. Higgs*, Vol. 13 (1981)

Action for the '80s: A Political, Professional, and Public Program for Foreign Language Education, *ed. Phillips*, Vol. 12 (1980)

The New Imperative: Expanding the Horizons of Foreign Language Education, *ed. Phillips*, Vol. 11 (1979)

Building on Experience—Building for Success, *ed. Phillips*, Vol. 10 (1978)

The Language Connection: From the Classroom to the World, *ed. Phillips*, Vol. 9 (1977)

An Integrative Approach to Foreign Language Teaching: Choosing Among the Options, *eds. Jarvis and Omaggio*, Vol. 8 (1976)

Perspective: A New Freedom, *ed. Jarvis*, Vol. 7 (1975)

The Challenge of Communication, *ed. Jarvis*, Vol. 6 (1974)

Foreign Language Education: A Reappraisal, *eds. Lange and James*, Vol. 4 (1972)

Foreign Language Education: An Overview, *ed. Birkmaier*, Vol. 1 (1969)

Professional Resources

A TESOL Professional Anthology: Culture

A TESOL Professional Anthology: Grammar and Composition

A TESOL Professional Anthology: Listening, Speaking, and Reading

ABC's of Languages and Linguistics

Award-Winning Foreign Language Programs: Prescriptions for Success, *Sims and Hammond*

Complete Guide to Exploratory Foreign Language Programs, *Kennedy and de Lorenzo*

Individualized Foreign Language Instruction, *Grittner and LaLeike*

Living in Latin America: A Case Study in Cross-Cultural Communication, *Gorden*

Oral Communication Testing, *Linder*

Practical Handbook to Foreign Language Elementary Programs, *Lipton*

Teaching Culture: Strategies for Intercultural Communication, *Seelye*

Teaching French: A Practical Guide, *Rivers*

Teaching German: A Practical Guide, *Rivers, et al.*

Teaching Spanish: A Practical Guide, *Rivers, et al.*

Transcription and Transliteration, *Wellisch*

 For further information or a current catalog, write:
National Textbook Company
4255 West Touhy Avenue
Lincolnwood, Illinois 60646-1975 U.S.A.